LANGUAGE AND IMAGERY IN THE OLD TESTAMENT

LANGUAGE AND IMAGERY IN THE OLD TESTAMENT

J.C.L. GIBSON

HENDRICKSON
PUBLISHERS

Hendrickson Publishers, Inc.
P.O. Box 3473
Peabody, Massachusetts 01961-3473

Language and Imagery in the Old Testament
ISBN 1-56563-090-4

First published in Great Britain 1998 by Society for Promoting Christian Knowledge, Holy Trinity Church, Marylebone Road, London NW1 4DU.

Hendrickson Publishers' edition is published by arrangement with SPCK.

Printed in the United States of America

First printing — November 1998

Cover: Details from the cover of the second Golden Book of the Jewish National Fund. Made by Bezalel artists. Jerusalem, 1913.
Photo: Ya'akov Brill, Beth Hatefutsoth.
Keren Kayemeth LeIsrael (JNF), Jerusalem/courtesy of Beth Hatefutsoth, Tel Aviv.
Special thanks to the Beth Hatefutsoth, The Nahum Goldmann Museum of the Jewish Diaspora, Tel Aviv.

CONTENTS

PREFACE

THE OLD TESTAMENT or, as it is called by Jews, Tanak (an acronym, in Hebrew, of the fuller title, 'The Law, the Prophets and the Writings') can be a cantankerous and off-putting body of literature, capable of causing not a little embarrassment to the two religions which have adopted it as their Scriptures, and frequently attracting opprobrium in the secular world; yet it is also highly seductive and moving, illumining for adherents of these religions the human predicament and how it may be alleviated, and even on occasion tempting some on the outside to wish they had such a faith. A chief reason for this two-way reaction to it is the power of its writing. It is on this rhetorical aspect of the Old Testament that I wish to lay most stress in the present volume, the way its message is given literary expression, the distinctive wording its authors employ, and the imaginative resources on which they draw. It is meant as a guide, not only to those who are accustomed to hearing the Old Testament read out to them in worship, but to that wider public who are intrigued by its enormous influence on indigenous languages and literatures and wonder why this should be so.

Ideally this kind of study should be based on the Hebrew text or, the next best thing, on the translation in any particular language which most faithfully reproduces its literary strengths. For speakers of English this is still, I believe, the Authorized or King James Version, but alas! its language is now rather archaic, and its renderings too often erroneous and too heavily Christianized. By way of compromise, quotations in this book are taken from the Revised Standard Version (Common Bible), which is a modern and reasonably reliable translation and has the added virtue of preserving links with the Authorized Version, of which it is a revision of a revision. I hope nonetheless that readers will have the Authorized Version by their side, and also will not be averse to consulting a range of modern translations, Christian and Jewish; for comparing versions is an excellent way for those who have no Hebrew of alerting their critical and appreciative antennae.

One or two remarks to set the scene are in order. The Old Testament is ignorant of the kind of philosophically angled discourse beloved of today's theologians and biblical scholars, a type of writing which had not yet been invented when it was first composed. It was addressed, on the contrary, to ordinary folks, and it employed the common genres available at that time: narrative, lyric, oracular, proverbial, encomium (praise), hortatory, didactic. Furthermore, it was first delivered orally, the stories being for public telling, the prophecies for preaching, the proverbs for handing down in the family or clan, the psalms for singing in the temple; and it was only written down later for preservation, though even then its primary purpose was to be read aloud among the people. In the process of writing down editorial activity was considerable, and many changes were made, but these should not be exaggerated. An ancient rhetoric still shines through, adapted of course to a new faith but not to that new faith in the various forms, Jewish or Christian, it was in the future to take. The thought-world that informs the Old Testament and the words it uses to express itself are those of a bygone age.

The book opens with a chapter on the 'energies' of the Hebrew language, and follows it with one on the difficulties encountered, even by Hebrew speakers, in adequately describing God. Then come two chapters on the rhetoric of the different Old Testament genres, prose or poetry, and the literary strategies its writers developed to persuade or challenge their audiences; and one on the role which myth, nowadays an outmoded genre, played in such rhetoric. Finally, there are two chapters on the imagery of the Old Testament, centring respectively on images of God and images of humanity. I hope that this sketch will increase readers' appreciation of the literary skill with which it clothed its message and enable them to close with a vision which, warts and all, can still awaken the atrophied imaginations of an unseeing age, and do something to heal its hurt.

The book is dedicated to the students I taught at New College for nearly a third of a century and tried to introduce to the magic appeal of a literature which is more than a compendium of religious belief and conduct. Perhaps some of them caught the strains of its music as they struggled with their Hebrew verbs or wrestled with its problematic doctrines.

New College, Edinburgh   John C. L. Gibson

− 1 −

THE ENERGIES OF
THE HEBREW LANGUAGE

L ET US BEGIN by citing a paragraph describing ancient
Hebrew by a famous Scottish Old Testament critic of
former years, Sir George Adam Smith:

> Few abstract terms exist in ancient Hebrew and no
> compound words. Abstractions and constructive power are
> almost as absent from the grammar and syntax as from the
> vocabulary. That subordination of clause to clause in which
> the subtlety and flexibility of other languages appear is
> hardly found, but to the end, both in prose and verse, the
> clauses are almost invariably strung together by the bare
> copulas *and* or *then* in a co-ordination which requires both
> skill and spirit to redeem it from monotony. (G. A. Smith, in
> E. R. Bevan and C. Singer (eds.), *The Legacy of Israel*, Clar-
> endon Press 1927, p. 11)

This rather flowery description highlights two basic characteristics of biblical Hebrew: lack of abstract terms and linking
together of clauses by 'and' (by 'then' the writer is evidently
thinking of the common English alternative of 'and' in narrative; there is no Hebrew 'then' of this kind). But if we are
strictly accurate, these two features do not tell us about the
Hebrew language itself so much as about, on the one hand, the
fact that Hebrew culture at the time the biblical books were
written had not yet developed the capacity to think philosophically and, on the other hand, the fondness of the Old
Testament writers for simple narrative and poetic style. One
could say much the same about Sir Patrick Spens and the early
Scottish ballads – hardly any abstract terms and a simplistic
poetic narrative style. But there is a difference. By the time the
Scottish ballads were composed, there did exist in the Scots
language many abstract terms and a variety of complicated

1

writing styles. You could choose which to use according to the literary activity in which you were engaged, and you would not choose the ballad style for writing, say, theological treatises. In ancient Israel, however, there were only narrative and poetry for literary purposes, and that obviously – for the Old Testament is full of stories and poems – included writing about religion. The writers of the Old Testament were not theologians like the professionals who hold teaching posts in our faculties and departments of Divinity and Theology. We must not make the mistake of supposing that they really thought like us but that, due to the fact that they were addressing unlettered audiences, they chose to put things more simply than they would have liked to. They were people of their age no less than their audiences, and they had no choice in the matter.

But to the points mentioned by Sir George, to which several more may be added.

Co-ordination by 'and'

Co-ordination – the use of clauses with 'and' rather than of clauses with 'if, when, until, although and so forth' – is, if not exactly a characteristic of Hebrew language as such, certainly a basic feature of Old Testament style. We might compare the opening of lines of Genesis as between the original Hebrew and some English translations. In the first five verses there are in the Hebrew eleven 'ands' linking clauses (as distinct from those linking words), of which all but one are reproduced in the Authorized Version (AV):

> 1. In the beginning God created the heaven and the earth. 2. *And* the earth was without form, and void: *and* darkness was upon the face of the deep. *And* the Spirit of God moved upon the face of the waters. 3. *And* God said, Let there be light *and* there was light. 4. *And* God saw the light, that it was good: *and* God divided the light from the darkness. 5. *And* God called the light Day, *and* the darkness he called Night. *And* the evening and the morning were the first day.

The one not reproduced is in the last sentence, which consists of two clauses in Hebrew, literally '*And* there was evening, *and* there was morning, one day.'

The Revised Standard Version (RSV), which stands in the AV tradition, has nine, two less than the Hebrew and one less than the AV:

> 1. In the beginning God created the heavens and the earth. 2. The earth was without form and void, *and* darkness was upon the face of the deep; *and* the Spirit of God was moving over the face of the waters. 3. *And* God said, 'Let there be light'; *and* there was light. 4. *And* God saw that the light was good; *and* God separated the light from the darkness. 5. God called the light Day, *and* the darkness he called Night. *And* there was evening, *and* there was morning, one day.

It begins verse 2 and 5 without 'and', but interestingly retains at the end of verse 5 the one in the Hebrew text which the AV left out.

The New English Bible (NEB), however, a new version from modern times, has only five:

> 1. In the beginning of creation, when God made heaven and earth, 2. the earth was without form and void; with darkness over the face of the abyss, and a mighty wind that swept over the surface of the waters. 3. God said, 'Let there be light', *and* there was light; 4. *and* God saw that the light was good, *and* he separated light from darkness. 5. He called the light day, *and* the darkness night. So evening came, *and* morning came, the first day.

It uses a clause with 'when' in verse 1, beginning the main clause at verse 2, but continuing it with the subordinations 'with darkness over' and '(with) a mighty wind that swept' (the 'and' now joining two phrases); it omits 'and' at the start of verses 3 and 5 (incidentally substituting 'he' for 'God' at the start of verse 5); and it has 'so' instead of 'and' in the second part of verse 5 though, like the RSV, it keeps in that half-verse the 'and' which the AV did not have.

What the NEB and to a lesser extent the RSV are doing, of course, is to follow normal English prose style, avoiding beginning a sentence with 'and', using alternatives like 'so', and breaking up the succession of 'ands' by various means of subordination. This is doubtless the right way to go about translating, but for our purposes it is fortunate that the AV is more faithful to the original Hebrew (as it is in other respects), and its evidence is welcome. There is no doubt that co-ordination of clauses by means of 'and' is a distinctive mark of the Hebrew language in biblical times.

But we cannot leave it at that; the statement requires modification. It does not take into account the numerous ways in which 'and' is disposed in Hebrew; for instance, it has different forms in past narrative and in future discourse, which distinguish these genres from each other and from direct speech or descriptions in the present. Also, the order of words in the clause following 'and' can be crucial; the usual word order in Hebrew is verb first then subject, but the subject often comes first, and this changes the meaning. Thus in Genesis 1.2 'and' is immediately succeeded by the nouns 'earth', 'darkness', 'Spirit of God' because the clauses are not continuous, but circumstantial, describing the conditions before the creation began. The first narrative portion opens at verse 3 with the clause 'And God said', and it begins with one of the special 'ands' and the verb first. Another construction which breaks the narrative flow is the chiasmus, in which the second of two clauses is on the same time-scale as the first and its close connection with the first is indicated in Hebrew by reversing the word order. The AV and RSV partially reproduce this order in Genesis 1.5 ('and the darkness he called Night'), but not the NEB, which ignores it as English translations commonly do.

In short, English is able to render the 'ands', though the result is quaint, for it would more often vary them by another conjunction like 'so' or 'then', or by omitting them altogether, or by introducing a subordination. But English cannot reproduce the different forms of 'and' in Hebrew or, except occasionally, the word order that follows the 'and'; it therefore misses the variety and flexibility of construction which in Hebrew accompany that small co-ordinator. Sir George is right about the frequency with which 'and' is used in Hebrew, but he is wrong about its monotony. He is, in making his judgement, not really basing himself on Hebrew syntax but on how it appears in English dress.

Lack of abstract terms

The other feature of Hebrew noticed in the quote from Sir George was its lack of abstract terms. This is in fact a truer observation than his first. Many centuries were to pass before Hebrew developed an armoury of abstract terms for the doing of philosophy or theology. In the Old Testament period Hebrew had no words, for instance, for 'creation' and 'providence', but had to speak, as Genesis 1.1 does, of God creating the heavens and the earth or, as Genesis 8.21 does, of God promising never to curse the ground again. But even where in English translation an abstract term is used, there is often not one there in Hebrew.

A good example is the word translated 'justice' in our modern versions, as in Amos 5.24:

> But let justice roll down like waters,
> And righteousness like an ever-flowing stream.

'Justice' is in the AV more accurately 'judgment', showing that the activity of making decisions about right and wrong is a more prominent ingredient in the word's meaning than any philosophical notion of what is involved in the concept of justice. Similarly, the second word used by Amos, 'righteousness', is in origin a legal term, the righteous man being the one declared to be in the right, pronounced innocent, because he behaves in an innocent or proper way, the righteous judge the one who conducts the case fairly, the righteous king the one who acts as a king should (or, in some contexts, the one who is the legitimate or lawful king), the righteous God the one who governs and disposes the world rightly. It is, in other words, always connected with someone's status or behaviour and not with an abstract idea. In the context in Amos with its attacks on social misbehaviour, the two words commend the proper conduct of law and the proper treatment of the underprivileged in a corrupt nation.

Even the word 'everlasting' joined with 'stream' in Amos has to be watched. The AV has 'mighty', which is weak; the NEB has 'ever-flowing', which is more like it; 'perennial' might be even better. The reference is to the drying up of wadis and streams during the summer season in a hot country, a very concrete allusion which has nothing to do with eternity, but with making the point that God's activity in doing right did not cease in the summer – nor should his people's. It is in fact doubtful whether the ancient Hebrews had any idea of 'eternity' in our sense; all the Hebrew words translated 'for ever', 'to all eternity', and so forth probably mean is a very long time, either forwards or backwards; compare the common phrase 'from everlasting to everlasting' (e.g. Ps. 103.17).

Some other examples. The word translated 'spirit' also means 'wind', and therefore has behind it an almost physical nuance of movement and uncertainty; thus in Genesis 1.2 the NEB has 'a mighty (i.e. godlike) wind' instead of the AV's 'Spirit of God', the point at issue being the rather important one of whether God was present in the original chaos or only entered it when he uttered his *fiat*, 'Let there be light'. It is interesting that the Revised English Bible has gone back to 'Spirit of God', having changed its mind on the issue. Another example is the magical phrase 'in the beauty of holiness' (Ps. 96.9, AV), where the enchanting but rather meaningless 'beauty' probably denotes more precisely 'garments', 'array' or possibly, on the strength of a Ugaritic word, something like 'theophany', that is, 'at his appearance in holiness' or similar. Even the word 'holiness', which in the Old Testament carries the broad connotation 'belonging to the divine sphere', may have behind it the concrete sense of light or purity. A final example is provided by the frequent phrases which speak of God's 'counsel' or purpose. When we learn that the same word can be translated 'council', we realize that again something physical is involved, namely the heavenly council which is met with at the beginning of the Book of Job, where God is pictured consulting with his angels ('sons of God' is what the Hebrew has) about what to do with Job. And so we could go on.

But there is one thing we must not do, and that is to confuse the inability of the Israelites to think abstractly with an inability to think profoundly. The writers of the Old Testament were not men of today; they did not employ a complicated philosophical or technical terminology, but to get over what they were trying to say had to use in the main stories and poems.

Prominence of direct speech

A third basic feature of Old Testament language (or, if you like, style), not cited by Sir George, is its penchant for direct speech. By this I do not simply mean the prominence of conversation in the biblical stories, though that is important, for example, for characterization, giving the opinion of the participants on what is happening (see Chapter 3, p. 47), but cases like Genesis 1 where God is not speaking to anyone: 'And God said, Let there be light', and so forth. It is very doubtful whether there is any real thought here of creation by the Word, certainly not in the sense of the prologue to St John's Gospel. Probably the phrase means little more than that God decided within himself to create light, and did so (if not in the case of light, it is significant that with the following acts of creation it has to be specifically stated that he made as well as said). For we find similar statements frequently by human characters, for instance, Eve saying in Genesis 4.1, 'I have gotten a man with the help of the Lord' (or perhaps better, catching the arrogance of the moment, 'as well as the Lord'). It sounds more like a description of the thought processes of Eve than an address to Adam, who is not mentioned. Even in a highly polished literary composition like Ecclesiastes we have commonly 'I said to myself' (literally 'in my heart'), with the writer's arguments and conclusions following in direct speech.

It is essentially the same with communication between the divine and the human, God himself or his angel coming down to a man and addressing him straight, and the man replying, the whole scene striking us as distinctly naive and sometimes theologically questionable, for example, where God in the Garden calls out to Adam, 'Where are you?' (Gen. 3.9). We are much happier, and it seems some of the biblical writers themselves were when such divine–human communication is described less crudely, as when it happens in a dream. Thus Jacob after his dream at Bethel about a ladder between heaven and earth, in which God speaks to him, wakes up and says, 'Surely the Lord is in this place; and I did not know it' (Gen. 28.16). In other words, he realizes from what had happened that God had been in touch with him (though, significantly, Jacob's own conclusion is still directed at no one in particular). Phrases like 'the meditation of my heart' in Psalm 19.14 or even a passive construction like 'by them is thy servant warned' in verse 11 of the same psalm, are relatively uncommon in Hebrew. The two phrases indeed stand out in that psalm for their abstract and indirect quality; for it begins, 'The heavens are telling the glory of God', not 'show', not 'reflect', but speak it out.

7

In a real sense it could be said that the fundamental mode of revelation (another term which has no Hebrew counterpart) is in the Old Testament speech. God 'speaks' to men rather than the safer theological 'reveals himself to' them, and his created world 'declares' his glory rather than 'mediates' or 'discloses' it. In so far as we have taken such God-talk into our own theological discourse is a measure of the Old Testament's continuing influence in theology rather than theology's own choice; on the whole it would prefer to avoid it. But it cannot avoid it in biblical translation, which puts the claims about updating the Bible into some perspective. We can touch up the syntax by removing some of the 'ands' and we can modernize an archaic term here and there (by, for instance, saying 'you' for 'thou'), though preferably not by using too many abstractions. But we cannot make an ancient book modern.

Other features

There are other features of Old Testament language which deserve mention, though properly they derive not so much from the language as such as from the level of culture which its writers had attained. There is, for instance, the interesting fact, which causes translators no end of bother, that the Hebrews thought with their 'heart' (as in the phrase cited above from Ecclesiates) not with their head, and felt emotion in their 'bowels' or 'livers', as in Genesis 43.30 where the AV has Joseph's 'bowels did yearn upon his brother' (RSV 'his heart', NEB 'his feelings').

Or there are cosmological descriptions of heaven up there and of Sheol down there, to which one 'ascends' or in which he 'makes his bed' (Ps. 139.8), of the 'firmament' (something dome-like and solid) which had the waters 'under' it and 'above' it (Gen. 1.7), of God 'putting' or hanging the stars in the firmament (Gen. 1.17), of him 'setting a bound' for the waters (Ps. 104.9), of the 'pillars' (RSV 'foundations') holding up the (flat) earth (Job 38.4), of the 'windows' of heaven to let the rain through (Gen. 7.11), and so on. We tend to regard those descriptions as figurative, and so in a sense they are, being the product partly of ancient imagination touching up the bare accounts; but for the most part they were taken literally, that being the way it was believed the world was actually constructed, ancient science as it were; and it is almost impossible now for us to distinguish the two.

Or there are the many instances of the extravagance of Semitic address known to us also from *The Arabian Nights*, phrases like 'your servant' and 'my lord' for 'I' and 'you' when talking to a superior; compare 'your maidservant' (Ruth 2.13), 'Is your servant a dog, that ...?' (see AV 2 Kings 8.13). Or there is the fondness for using relational terms, literally perhaps in 'children of Israel' for the people as a whole, or 'son of man' for any human being, but surely metaphorical in 'sons of strangers' (AV Isa. 60.10), 'sons of flame' for sparks (Job 5.7), 'daughter of Zion' for the inhabitants of Jerusalem, not necessarily female (Isa. 1.8), 'the daughter of my people' for simply my people (AV Jer. 8.11), and so forth. Some of these phrases may indicate Hebrew's lack of adjectives (it has many fewer than English) rather than a particularly poetic turn of speech, though they strike our ears as very colourful.

Another habit of the biblical writers, dependent no doubt on tribal tradition, is giving etymologies of names that encapsulated the character of the people concerned. Female personal names in ancient Israel are usually connected with animals or flowers, for example, Deborah (a bee), Rachel (a ewe), Susannah (a lily), but male names are frequently little prayers, for example, Jacob, 'may he (God) follow at the heel' (of the child so-named to protect him), Israel, 'may God strive' (on behalf of the child); and the people must have known this. That these two names are given the interpretations 'he (Jacob) supplants' (Gen. 27.36) and 'he (Israel, or the people stemming from him) strives' (Gen. 32.28) is the result of intentionally false folk etymologies. The meaning of the divine name Yahweh is lost in the mists of time, though in Exodus 3 it is given the etymology 'I am that I am' or possibly 'I will be what I will be', but that is probably a folk etymology too, or perhaps rather a later scribal one if it is interpreted in terms of self-existence or revealing himself by what he does, two rather advanced ideas. The form of the word suggests it may have something to do with creation or 'causing to be', but we cannot be sure. All we can say is that (male) names were subject in ancient Israel to manipulation, and for us the meaning given them is the one that matters, since it is the one which is used in Scripture.

The linguistic features listed here, although their origin is

Hebrew anthropology, cosmology, social behaviour, popular etymologizing and so on, do lend a sort of distinctiveness to Old Testament language, and we should constantly be on the lookout for them, if only to remind ourselves that our ways of expressing ourselves in these matters are often very different.

Figures of speech or tropes

Which brings us to openly figurative language. The literature of the Old Testament, particularly its poetry, like other literatures often uses language for expressive or rhetorical purposes. The devices employed – metaphor, simile and the rest – all use words in other than their straightforward sense or in other than their normal kind of context. The images which we shall be examining in later chapters – those applied to God, to human beings, or to nature, evil and death – have such figures of speech, notably metaphor, at their heart. But for now some introductory comments may help us to appreciate them better.

First, many of the images and the figures that comprise them are conventional, the literature of the Old Testament being for the most part a public literature. It was accessible to far more than a bookish readership because, even in its written form, it is not far removed from its oral origin. It is the written record of stories, psalms, proverbs that were meant to be recited or sung. The figures of speech tend to become attached to the various genres, which are not all that many, or they are used across the genres to describe the same relatively limited range of people and institutions. It is not often that the original or unusual image is found, so prized among modern authors writing for a private readership. There are exceptions, notably the Book of Job, where we are in touch with an individual poet of extraordinary power. But on the whole it is an uneducated and listening rather than an élite book-buying and reading public that had to be pleased, and they preferred the well-worn and familiar to the surprising and new.

Second and consequently, it is a people's understanding of their physical and intellectual environment that is reflected in the figures of speech – their conception of the universe, not ours, their reaction to the geography and flora and fauna of Palestine, not ours, their experience of human existence, so short in its life-expectancy and subject to dreadful diseases,

their social organization and customs, not ours, their ideas of
God and how he should be served, not ours – and not always
even (with, for instance, their openness to mythology) those of
the orthodox among them. Israel's imaginative thinking therefore brings before us many pictures which are attractive and
helpful to us, as of God as a shepherd tending his sheep, but
due to the difference in culture, not a few which we find off-
putting and not at all helpful.

It may simply be a matter of taste. Take these lines from the
Song of Songs where the lover describes his beloved:

> Behold, you are beautiful, my love,
>   behold, you are beautiful!
> Your eyes are doves,
>   behind your veil.
> Your hair is like a flock of goats,
>   moving down the slopes of Gilead.
> Your teeth are like a flock of shorn ewes
>   that have come up from the washing.
>
>   . . .
>
> Your neck is like the tower of David,
>   built for an arsenal,
> whereon hang a thousand bucklers,
>   all of them shields of warriors.
> Your two breasts are like two fawns,
>   twins of a gazelle,
>   that feed among the lilies.
>   (Song of Sol. 4.1–2, 4–5)

It is difficult to conceive of a western girl being moved by such
comparisons!

But sometimes it is more than a matter of taste. The very
Song of Songs which we have quoted is a case in point. It
celebrates love between the sexes in a kind of masque of
courtship and marriage, being modelled on wedding poetry
quite familiar to village life in ancient Israel. But later, both in
Judaism and even more in Christianity, sexual love was
frowned upon, and it was commonly allegorized as reflecting
the love between God and his people or, in Christian circles,
between Christ and his Church. That allegorizing indeed may

have been the reason why it gained entry into the canon of Scripture. In these laxer days it can be accepted for what it is, and we are more likely to be glad than uncomfortable that it found a place in the Bible.

We are not, on the contrary, so likely to approve of the way women are in general treated in the Bible, though let us not forget that, for all its patriarchal ways, they were accorded an honoured place in society. A good example of this is the picture of the ideal housewife in Proverbs chapter 31, rising in the middle of the night to see to the needs of her household and blessed by her husband and family. But it was a limited honour, and modern society is not on the whole impressed. In scriptural times sons were more highly prized than daughters, wives who did not bear children were despised and, in legal terms at any rate, they were little more than chattels of their husbands. We cannot go back to these days and model woman's position in our society on the Scriptures; and metaphors drawn from the Bible's way of life in this respect have to be treated with suspicion and kid gloves. It is the same with a 'spare the rod and spoil the child' attitude to the upbringing of the young, as in the Book of Proverbs.

Another area of imaginative language which bulks large in the Old Testament but is often distressing to modern susceptibilities is that drawn from warfare, especially when God's approval is constantly sought and given. In the old poem in Exodus 15, which takes pride in the exodus, God is actually called a 'man of war'. We can thrill to that miraculous event as we do to the battle of Marathon or, in more recent times, to the battle of Britain, when a few took on many, but why the wallowing in warfare and the triumphalism shown in Israel's victory? The Israelites were undoubtedly a warlike people, always having to fight for their lives against hostile neighbours; and like it or not we have to put up with descriptions of sieges and of the clash of arms, and with the use of figures drawn from these to illumine the character of their God, or what even we ourselves call the 'battle of life'. Wars and rumours of wars are everywhere in Scripture, and it is difficult to see us entirely dropping metaphors from that activity from our religious language. But that it constitutes a real problem for this age cannot be denied.

My third point may mitigate some of the criticisms levelled at the Old Testament and its imagery. I shall be mentioning it again with regard to its pictures of the deity (see Chapter 2). It is that an image by the comparison it evokes is partial; it centres on only one aspect of the comparison and ignores other aspects. We should not erect a figure of speech, nice or nasty, into a doctrine or a treatise, remembering that ancient Israel did what we call theology poetically rather than conceptually. This often gives the impression that the people of Israel thought in blacks and whites. To judge by their literature they veered from exaltation to despair, from loyalty to apostasy, from magnanimity to cruelty, almost at the drop of a hat. I have little doubt that they would have made a more coherent and proportioned job of expressing themselves if they had had the literary means and had confined themselves to the careful language of theology. But that is not the way figurative language works, but in brief and sudden flashes of insight; people at the metaphorical stage of human development had no balanced academic language to communicate with, in religion as in other things.

We may think that story and song, or oracular or lyrical or even didactic poetry are not the best medium for considered theology; they grasp the moment rather than the whole, they express feelings and emotions rather than thought, they are replete with contradictions, they are tied to the scenery and mores of ancient Palestine. Yet they have their own kind of power and attraction. I suspect that professional theologians do not like the Bible all that much. It is too folksy and too intolerant, too biased, imaginative rather than cerebral. They read it because it is their chief source-book for the events and people who gave them their faith, but they change its language quickly into their more acceptable doctrinal and philosophical talk; and many ordinary believers try to follow them. Not so many respond imaginatively to Scripture or at any rate not when they are on their best theological behaviour. But if they examine honestly their attitude to Scripture 'behind the scenes', as it were, they may admit that what above all it gives them is not doctrinal 'facts' to ponder, but something more valuable, an imaginative vision of God and his dealings with human beings to which to cling. It is the stories and poetry of Scripture and especially perhaps its figurative language which create that vision. In other areas of our reading experience we know all about cerebral language, yet even in this age we prefer novels and poems. We are nearer the metaphorical age of human thought than we admit, and in our heart of hearts we know that it is not facts and doctrines, but the vision of story and poetry and imagery that sustains our faith – or makes us regret that we do not have one.

Three specific tropes

The imagery of the Old Testament will be our chief concern in several other chapters, but I would like in this introductory chapter to finish by saying a little about three specific modes of figurative expression which will not as such be before us again. Each is at home in all kinds of ancient Hebrew writing. They are hyperbole, personification and irony.

Hyperbole

This is a distinctive mark of Semitic speech in general quite apart from the Hebrew Bible. It often strikes westerners as rather crude compared with the understatements (litotes) which are more to their taste. But the Old Testament in its oriental fashion habitually lets its hair down and exaggerates and overstates with considerable aplomb.

In the promise to Abraham his descendants will not only be numerous but like the sand of the sea or the stars of heaven. Numbers in the Old Testament are frequently talked up; the listeners must have known that there were many fewer than 600,000 taking part in the exodus, but that kind of detail underscored the belief that heaven was on their side (as in Judg. 5.20 the 'stars in their courses', AV, fought against Sisera). They were well aware that it was in reality a pretty small and bedraggled host that escaped from Pharaoh, for they are told elsewhere that Yahweh did all the fighting and Israel's role was merely to spectate (Exod. 14.14); but such 'facts' hardly seem to matter. Equally, the ages of the pre-diluvian patriarchs (Methuselah at 969 is the oldest; Gen. 5.27) are impossible, but they were intended to make it clear that in those days, unlike now, men were really men ('there were giants in the earth' then; 6.4, AV). Again, prominent throughout Scripture is the word 'all'; 'all Israel' attended at Mt Carmel to witness Elijah's contest with the prophets of Baal (1 Kings 18.19), and Absalom 'went in' to his father's concubines in the sight of 'all Israel' (2 Sam. 16.22). In neither case was this true in a literal sense; rather a large and representative body were present at Mt Carmel while, in Absalom's case, his rebellious act quickly became known throughout the country. But hyperbole added to the importance of the one event, and to the horror felt at the other.

Another example of hyperbole is the way natural phenomena are exploited for effect. Jeremiah (4.23ff.) describes the results of an invasion in terms that suggest primaeval chaos had returned (note the phrase 'waste and void' as in Gen. 1.2):

> I looked on the earth, and lo, it was waste and void;
>   and to the heavens, and they had no light.
> I looked on the mountains, and lo, they were quaking,
>   and all the hills moved to and fro.
> I looked, and lo, there was no man,
>   and all the birds of the air had fled.
> I looked, and lo, the fruitful land was a desert,
>   and all its cities were laid in ruins.

Psalm 18.7ff. uses similar language to describe the appearance of God to an individual worshipper in the temple, and Isaiah 40.3ff. exaggerates the march of God leading his exiles home to Jerusalem in a veritable new exodus: 'every valley shall be lifted up and every mountain and hill be made low'.

Personal emotions are vastly overdone, for example:

> Jacob: 'you would bring down my grey hairs with sorrow to Sheol'. (Gen. 42.38)
>
> the psalmist: 'I am a worm, and no man'. (Ps. 22.6)
>
> Job: 'Job arose, and rent his robe, and shaved his head, and fell upon the ground'. (Job 1.20)
>
> Hezekiah: 'My dwelling is plucked up and removed from me like a shepherd's tent; like a weaver I have rolled up my life; he cuts me off from the loom'. (Isa. 38.12)

The wit of Proverbs supplies many examples of hyperbole:

> Like vinegar to the teeth, and smoke to the eyes,
>   so is the sluggard to those who send him. (10.26)

> It is better to live in a corner of the housetop,
>   than in a house shared with a contentious woman. (25.24)

Finally, a whole book like Esther can use hyperbole almost as a narrative device, allied with macabre humour and not a little irony; Esther is promised whatever gift she may desire up to 'half my kingdom' (as in many a fairy-tale), and the gallows which Haman meant for Mordecai, (Esth. 7.9–10), and on which he met his own demise, were 'fifty cubits' (seventy-five feet!) high. There are similar exaggerations in the stories in the first half of the Book of Daniel, also about a Jew living under foreign domination, for example, the furnace heated to seven times its normal (Dan. 3.19). Such details pointed up the threat the people were under and the miraculous escapes they experienced.

At any rate, it would be foolish to take the exaggerations of the Old Testament at their face value for we would then quite miss their point. Not a few unimaginative believers today, sold on the 'truth' of the Bible, seem unable to avoid falling into that trap.

Personification

In personification an inanimate object or entity or an animal (or a god, or God) is spoken of as though it or he were a human person with human characteristics.

Balaam's ass talks and argues in Numbers 22.28, as does the serpent in Genesis 2 and 3 (and as in general animals do in fables). In Psalm 96 the heavens are glad and the earth rejoices at the Lord's coming, the sea roars, the field exults and all the trees of the wood sing for joy; in Psalm 98.8 the floods clap their hands; in Psalm 148 the whole of created nature is called upon to praise the Lord. In Job 17.14 rottenness is addressed as father and worms as sister and brother; Job 18.13–14 speaks of 'the first-born of death' consuming the wicked man's limbs and accords to the figure of death (a former god?), before whom he will be hauled, the title 'king of terrors'. In Habakkuk 2.11 the stones cry out from the wall, and the beams from the woodwork respond. In Proverbs 8.10 Lady Wisdom calls out to men on the heights beside the way: 'Take my instruction instead of silver, and knowledge rather than choice gold', and goes on to speak of herself as helping God in creation, while in the previous chapter Lady Folly, looking out of her window, tempts the young men as they pass or, dressed as a harlot, waits at the corner to seduce them.

Sometimes personification is extended to groups of people like nations or tribes, the group being regarded as a single person. Thus Jerusalem is addressed as a female, as in Isaiah 40.2:

> Speak tenderly to Jerusalem,
>   and cry to her
> that her warfare is ended,
>   that her iniquity is pardoned.

and Israel (or Jacob) as a male, as in Hosea 11.1:

> When Israel was a child, I loved him;
>   and out of Egypt I called my son.

the two pictures nicely complementing one another. Probably the servant of Isaiah 53 is a personification of Israel as a nation, and not an individual like the coming Messiah or even, as the New Testament frequently implies, Jesus of Nazareth. Even the gods in council can be addressed as though they had real power and being, contrary to the usual picture of them as mere idols of stone and wood, which cannot move from their place (Isa. 46.5ff.). Thus in Psalm 82.6–7 God says to the other deities, 'You are gods, sons of the Most High, all of you; nevertheless, you shall die like men, and fall like any prince.' (See further Chapter 2.)

With such an abundance of personification in the Old Testament, it is tempting to explain the practice by its polytheistic background with its habit of deifying all sorts of natural and other phenomena; but the beliefs of Israel's neighbours, not to mention Israel's monotheism, were far beyond that primitive stage. The instances above in Job 18 (death) and Psalm 82 (council of gods) may well have a mythical origin (see Chapter 5), but in other cases it is much more likely that the figures go back to the conventions of folk tales (Balaam's ass) or the universal custom of calling tribes after their eponymous ancestors (Israel, Jacob), if they are not simply due to the writer's imagination at work. But whatever the reason, there is no doubt that personification is found everywhere in the Old

Testament, probably more so than in modern literature, and is part and parcel of its literary and imaginative baggage.

Irony

There is more irony in the Old Testament than we think. The rather straight-faced piety of Bible readers often gets in the way, and we do not recognize it as we might, at least if we are Christian readers; Jewish readers are more open to it.

The irony may be on a relatively small scale and reside in a spoken sentence or two, as when Rachel sits on a camel on top of Laban's household gods while her father searches frantically through the house, and sweetly says that she cannot rise, 'for the way of women is upon me' (Gen. 31.34–5) – the listeners are meant to laugh at the incongruity of the picture. A similar example comes from the Book of Amos; the prophet is preaching at Bethel, the chief sanctuary of the northern kingdom (Israel) and lambasts the surrounding nations and then Judah, the southern kingdom, and finally he homes in on Israel – we can see the listeners smiling in approval at the beginning but then suddenly breaking out in anger as they realize that they are included in the judgement too.

Or it may be thematic, as the people in general gradually, as Scripture unwinds, are reminded of the ironies surrounding their central beliefs of promise, election and providence. In Genesis the venal Esau turns out to be a better man in the end than Jacob, forgiving his brother, but it is the roguish Jacob who is chosen. In Samuel the bumbling but hardly wicked Saul has the kingdom removed from him, whereas the scheming and selfish David gets away (literally in Uriah's case) with murder and dies peacefully in his bed, honoured everywhere and founder of a dynasty – but he was the Lord's anointed. There is the same thematic irony in the prophets, who have to announce doom on God's chosen people when they were expecting success. And in the Wisdom literature, as Job and Ecclesiastes take apart the traditional view of the Book of Proverbs that the righteous will be rewarded and the wicked punished. Job suffers when he should have prospered, and Ecclesiastes' favourite word 'vanity', so remorselessly applied to all human activities and hopes, could almost be a Hebrew equivalent of 'irony'.

A remarkable example of thematic irony is the Book of Jonah, as Israel's attachment to its special status is savagely lampooned by the story of a prophet who, when instructed to preach to Nineveh, the Assyrian capital, tries every trick to escape from his commission, and even when he is cast up by the 'great fish' at the very city he had been avoiding, carries out his task reluctantly, complaining all the while – yet Nineveh repents in sackcloth and ashes. So vividly and indeed humorously is the scene portrayed that if it had been a play instead of a story, the audience would have been rolling in the aisles. Yet the irony is mordant too; we only need to read the short Book of Nahum to see how deep went the hatred of the Assyrians among the Israelites, and how they looked forward to Niniveh's utter annihilation. It is the irony of grace that we meet in the Book of Jonah, encompassing not only Israel but Israel's enemies, and even the cattle in the fields (Jonah 4.11); in the last analysis it is incomprehensible, and only irony makes it bearable.

Allied to situational irony is what is called dramatic irony, which occurs when an audience at a play or the readers of a book know more about what is going on than the characters on the stage or in the story. This occurs not a few times in the Old Testament, as when first the brothers of Joseph and then, in Egypt, Joseph himself think they are in charge of events, but in the end find that only God behind the scenes was really in charge. It is even clearer in the Book of Job; both the members of the heavenly court at the beginning and, of course, the readers, know that Job is a good man being put through the mill by God and his side-kick Satan, but neither Job nor his friends know this but only have what happens to him in real life to go by.

But perhaps the most perturbing and, when one considers Jewish humour, the most characteristic feature of Old Testament irony is that it is irony at the expense of God. Think of Topol's plea in *Fiddler on the Roof*, 'Would it spoil some vast, eternal plan, if I were a wealthy man?' The second half of Job 7 has several examples of this kind. In 7.12 Job complains, 'Am I the sea, or a sea monster, that thou settest a guard over me?', in other words, am I the fabled monster of the primaeval deep, who has to be chained up, in case I should escape and cause another flood? In 7.17–18 there is a fierce parody of Psalm 8,

'What is man, that thou dost make so much of him ... dost visit him every morning, and test him every moment?' Pious people like the psalmist or Job's three friends might rejoice in God's visiting him with his consolation, but to Job it was more like a sergeant-major hectoring him on the parade ground, never giving him a second's breathing space 'to swallow my spittle'. In 7.20 there is a second parody of psalms language, 'thou watcher of men'; the same word is used at least a dozen times in the Psalms of God watching over or preserving his worshippers. Most scurrilous of all is 7.21, 'Why dost thou not pardon my transgression?', reminding us of the blasphemy of the philosopher Heine (or the Empress Catherine of Russia, who is also credited with the saying), *Le bon Dieu me pardonera, c'est son métier* ('The good God will forgive me, that's his business'). Lastly, in the same verse, is Job's appeal to God to let him lie in the earth, for then 'thou wilt seek me, but I shall not be (there)'.

I suppose one is not surprised at such irony in the Book of Job, as Job is constantly impugning the divine justice; but it is there elsewhere too. It is there by implication in the way storyteller and poet frame their compositions; God's grace is almost invariably a source of amazement, sometimes consternation, and his favouritism is not only enjoyed, but called in question. Perhaps verbally it is not so common; but let us consider, in addition to the examples quoted from Job, forefather Abraham's objection in Genesis 18.25, 'Far be that from thee! Shall not the Judge of all the earth do right?', the subject of many a pious sermon, but in its context, as the scope of God's salvation is beaten down from fifty to forty to thirty to ten righteous inhabitants of Sodom and Gomorrah who might merit it (why not to one?), it is not without its dash of irony. God can, it seems, be bargained with, and made to live up (if we may so phrase it) to his better self. Irony and indeed humour at God's expense is really a form of protest and conceals the pain which God's perplexing ways bring to his worshippers.

These, then, are some of the ways in which the Hebrew language of the Old Testament shows itself – co-ordination of sentences rather than subordination, absence of abstract terms, a predilection for direct speech, vocabulary drawn from the people's daily life and experience, and a largely conventional, if powerful, use of figures of speech, three of the most characteristic being hyperbole, personification and irony. If we think the Old Testament worth studying, we have to come to terms with that particular language, as it was in Old Testament times and with its particular modes of expression, however unfamiliar, naive and out of date these may seem, and on not a few occasions, however offensive and hurtful; and we have to resist the temptation to touch up or modify them or reinterpret them in order to make them more congenial to our modern age. The Old Testament comes to us via an ancient people, and its writers first addressed that people, and only us through them. Especially has this to be remembered when they talk about God. We have looked at this in one or two places in the present chapter (the use of military metaphors to describe him, or of irony used at his expense). In the next we shall consider it further.

-2-

LANGUAGE ABOUT GOD
IN THE OLD TESTAMENT

THE WAY THE Old Testament writers speak about God can, as we have seen, often appear strange, and sometimes be perturbing to today's readers. I wish in this chapter to address two specific aspects of their God-talk which have this capacity in full measure: the predilection of the biblical writers for the wildest of anthropomorphisms, and their reluctance on numerous occasions to describe monotheism, supposedly their single most impressive achievement in the realm of religion, in what we would regard as a fitting manner.

The problem of anthropomorphisms

All God-talk, all theology, even ours, is metaphorical, describing God in terms that properly belong to the human sphere. It cannot be otherwise, as human words, like human thought, belong this side of creation, and cannot begin to describe its other side, God as he is in his own interior life. Such knowledge as we have of God is not of God as he is, but as he shows himself towards human beings. When we talk about God's word, we are saying that God communicates with us in a way similar to our speaking with each other. When we say that God saves, redeems, pities us, is our Father, our shepherd, our King, we are using metaphors or images drawn from human life and experience. In other words, we are using anthropomorphisms, ascribing to God human actions and human feelings.

Since the pictures evoked by the metaphors I have mentioned are pleasant ones, we do not usually think of them when we raise the problem of anthropomorphisms in the Old Testament. Rather, we tend to restrict the term to two kinds of description: first, *naive* ones, as when God like a potter makes man out of a lump of clay or takes a walk in the garden or holds conversations with snakes (Gen. 2–3); and second, *nasty* ones, which picture God giving way to the less admirable human passions, as when he is sorry that he created man and changes his mind (Gen. 6.6), or as when he displays jealousy (1 Kings 14.22) or military prowess (Exod. 15.3). These are the sort of pictures of God which lead to much scorn and criticism of the Old Testament. Usually, we either laugh at their primitiveness and blame the ancient Israelites for them, or we try to defend them by a process of theological sleight-of-hand: God is God, and cannot be judged by our standards. In short, we either judge him by our own standards (God must always be good and just as we conceive goodness and justice); or, contradicting ourselves, we justify the most human aspects of God by appealing to his difference from human beings. This will not do.

But let us now look in more detail at three particularly repulsive passages in the Old Testament, which more than most have activated the defensive antennae of today's religious people – one in which God tells a lie, one in which he is unfair, and one in which he is vindictive.

1. In Genesis chapter 2 God tells Adam and Eve that if they eat of the tree of knowledge, they shall die. Later the serpent tells Eve that they shall not die but their eyes shall be opened and they will become like God, knowing good and evil. Later again (Gen. 3.22) God admits that the serpent was right, 'Behold, the man has become like one of us, knowing good and evil'. The plain sense of this sequence is that God told a lie, or at any rate that he deceived Adam and Eve quite out-rageously. To make the sense otherwise we have to prevaricate: they didn't exactly die on the day they ate of the tree (which is what God said, Gen. 2.17) but became subject to death, and so on. But what are we doing here but rushing to God's defence? Though the Hebrews were seemingly not worried that God should tell a lie or deceive Adam and Eve, we today are; and to preserve our idea of God we have to twist the text.

2. The example of God being unfair is found in the incident of the hardening of Pharaoh's heart. Take the description in Exodus chapter 7. God says to Moses, 'I (will) make you as God to Pharaoh; ... and Aaron your brother shall tell Pharaoh to let the people of Israel go out of his land. But I will harden Pharaoh's heart, and ... Pharaoh will not listen to you; then I will lay my hand upon Egypt and bring forth ... my people ...

by great acts of judgment' (Exod. 7.1–4). As I understand this passage, it instructs Aaron to ask Pharaoh to let people go, then God hardens his heart so that he does not let them go, which gives God an excuse for clobbering Pharaoh for his hardness of heart. It hardly seems fair. Doubtless we would prefer to speak of Pharaoh hardening his own heart and meriting the plagues that come upon, and so sometimes does the writer (e.g. Exod. 8.32). But that is not what the Bible says in this passage. Again it seems that the Hebrews (at least here) saw nothing untoward about God hardening Pharaoh's heart and thereafter punishing him for it. But again people today are unable to stomach this notion and doctor the story in accordance with their own view of how God should behave.

3. The third example is illustrated by the first couple of chapters of the Book of Job. We not uncommonly interpret the trials sent on Job as God's testing of him. But that is not his purpose as it is described in the story as we have it. It begins with God boasting to Satan how blameless and upright his servant Job is. Satan makes the not unreasonable suggestion that a man so blessed with prosperity could hardly help being good, and asks 'Does Job fear God for naught?' (Job 1.9). This annoys God and he makes a wager with Satan that Job would remain faithful whatever the circumstances, and he specifically invites Satan to slay Job's servants and his sons and daughters, and later to infect him with loathsome diseases. This does not suggest to me that God was testing Job so much as that God wanted to score a petulant point off Satan, and in order to do this he is willing to sacrifice the old man's whole family. Vindictive does not seem to me at all too strong a word.

Now, in each of these examples of God behaving very unpleasantly indeed, I have simply spelled out what the Old Testament itself says. I have not read into the stories what is not there. I have also hinted that in order to make them acceptable to our modern ways of thinking about God, we have to do quite a bit of doctoring. It is we who read in what is not there; or, if we do not, we fall back on a dogmatic defence that will not have us questioning divine behaviour on the grounds that God is God and can do what he likes. The Old Testament may be rugged and pull no punches in its description of God, but it is at least consistent and avoids the sanctimoniousness in which we indulge.

There is a theological reason for, or at least explanation of, this way of speaking about God, though it hardly commends itself to us either. By and large the Old Testament accepts that God causes evil as well as good, that if you like he has built into the fabric of the universe a dualism of light and darkness, good and evil, and is therefore himself as much responsible for the one as for the other. God is always in control and at the end of the day evil is admitted to derive from him, for example:

The Lord kills and brings to life (1 Sam. 2.6)

The Spirit of the Lord departed from Saul, and an evil spirit from the Lord tormented him. (1 Sam. 16.14)

I am the Lord, and there is no other.
I form the light and create darkness,
   I make weal and create woe (Isa. 45.6–7)

Does a lion roar ... when he has no prey? ...
Does evil befall a city,
   unless the Lord has done it? (Amos 3.4–6)

This strict and frightening monotheism was, of course, formulated in reaction to a polytheistic environment, where the good and bad aspects of what the Greeks call fate were parcelled out among different deities. Ancient Israel had only one God, and she was not afraid to draw the corollary that he sent evil as well as good. On the contrary, the New Testament and later Judaism tend to remove evil from God's direct responsibility and assign it to the Devil or some other power. It is hardly to be wondered at that people today do not read what the Old Testament says, but what they think it says, and that when this is pointed out to them, they get perplexed and annoyed.

I began with the Old Testament language – its sometimes extremely free and perturbing descriptions of God in terms of the nastier human qualities – and I have linked these pictures with Old Testament theology – its ready acceptance that God is responsible for evil as well as good. Behind both lies its apprehension of God as absolutely transcendent and sovereign. But it is not the second problem as much as the first that in this chapter I am concerned with. It is not the origin of evil that we should here be considering, but the amazing freedom in general of the Old Testament's manner of speaking about God.

I have suggested on a literary level that this derives from its awareness that all descriptions of God are metaphorical, an awareness that is, if anything, more rather than less sophisticated than ours, since we tend to think that with our good metaphors we are describing God as he really is and that the odd or extravagant or unpleasant metaphors, which so abound in the Old Testament, alone constitute a problem for believers.

But there is more than this to be said. The passages we have been examining earlier are parts of imaginative stories, myths and legends, if you like, or parables; and these are in a real sense simply extended metaphors. What I am getting at is that if you put God in a story, and you want it to be a good story, he is almost bound to end up as both the good fairy and the big bad wolf. If in any of these stories God had not been the deceiver, the hardener of hearts, the initiator of suffering, then in each of them he would have been reacting to events, not in control of them, cleaning up messes for which he was not responsible. And so it would be in the story of salvation as a whole; human beings not God would be the prime mover, and God's role restricted to a nurse's binding up wounds or a fireman's putting out fires or a social worker's attending a twice-weekly clinic. Not that we should not use metaphors picturing God as a nurse or a fireman or a social worker – or, in biblical words, as a shepherd leading us through the valley, or a redeemer taking us out of pawn. He does act in such ways, and such images bring it home to our imaginations, the nasty as well as the nice. The essence of a striking metaphor is that only one aspect of the comparison holds good, and the essence of appreciating it is that we do not bring in other aspects. We should look for the salient point, and leave it at that; and even if we cannot find it, due to the strangeness of the literature or our own beliefs, we should remember that the ancient Israelites could, and did. The issue in biblical anthropomorphisms is understanding them, not approving or disapproving them.

The incomparability of Yahweh

The monotheism of the Old Testament has been in the previous section adduced as a possible explanation, not only for the Old

Testament's tendency to make God the originator of both good and evil, but for its fondness for widening the scope of its anthropomorphisms to include the nasty as well as the nice elements in the divine nature. But there is another kind of language about God in the Old Testament which seems to go the opposite way and give a measure of reality to other divine powers, and thus call in question the Old Testament's very attachment to monotheism. It too must derive from the polytheistic environment of ancient Israel, but instead of giving to the one God, Yahweh, the attributes of surrounding deities, it accords these deities at least a partial existence and a real power. This too is a rather perturbing use of language and needs examining.

In describing the nature and activity of Yahweh, some writers of the Old Testament were as apt to use language which strikes us as polytheistic as to use language which we would accept as monotheistic. Modern Old Testament scholarship, confronted with such a language mix, is uneasy; it senses a problem and, as is its academic wont, it looks for a historical solution. Monotheism becomes the final stage in a religious development which began with ancient Israel's religion being little different from the religions of their polytheistic neighbours. For the stage in between, the term 'henotheism' is the word often used; other gods might exist, but for Israel only one God mattered. I do not doubt that there is truth in this reading of the evidence; but it is by no means the whole truth. Left unasked is the question whether the ancient Israelites were as uncomfortable with the language mix I have mentioned as the modern scholar is. The answer must surely be that they were not. In this section, therefore, I would like to eschew too much historical probing, and simply look at Old Testament language in this regard as it comes to us. I am assuming, in effect, that these writers knew very well what they were doing when they combined in their description of Yahweh what we would regard as both polytheistic and monotheistic features.

Let us begin our investigation with the *Shema* (Deut. 6.4): 'Hear, O Israel: the Lord our God is one Lord.' (This confession of faith is known as the *Shema* from its opening word in Hebrew: *Shema* ('Hear').) Here at least it would seem that we have something unambiguously monotheistic. But the statement is not at all as clear in Hebrew as it appears to be in

English. 'The Lord' is a title which was at some point in Israel's history – we are not sure when – substituted for the actual name of Israel's God, Yahweh, which as time went on was considered too holy to say out loud. It is 'Yahweh' which is in the text. Moreover, as commonly in nominal sentences of this kind, there is no copula in Hebrew; 'is' has to be supplied by the translator as he thinks appropriate. Properly, therefore, the English translation I have cited (the RSV) ought to go, 'Yahweh our God is one Yahweh', which does not seem to me to mean very much. The most commonly suggested alternative is 'Yahweh our God, Yahweh is one', which keeps us pretty firmly within a monotheistic ambit. But equally possible is 'Yahweh our God, Yahweh is the only one', in which case the statement would rather be drawing attention to Yahweh's uniqueness as compared to other deities. A fourth possibility is 'Yahweh is our God, Yahweh alone'; and there also the existence of other gods is implicit, though the emphasis is on Yahweh's sole claim to Israel's allegiance.

I am inclined to favour the last of these translations, on the grounds that the *Shema* was a declaration of faith, intended to set Israel apart from other nations, an invitation to them to confess the God who had delivered their ancestors from Egypt and brought them to Sinai to hear his law. But I would not wish a nuance of Yahweh's distinctiveness over against other gods to be overlooked; it must be there too; for, as we shall shortly find out, a very large proportion of Old Testament descriptions of God contain an element of comparison with other gods, and in not a few of them the phraseology used can strike our modern ears as distinctly embarrassing.

One of the cooler of such descriptions, with which Deuter-onomy 6.4 must be linked, is the first of the Ten Command-ments which, with its preamble, reads (Exod. 20.2–3; Deut. 5.6–7) 'I am the Lord your God, who brought you out of the land of Egypt, out of the house of bondage. You shall have no other gods before me.' The people of Israel here also acknow-ledge their relationship to the deity who had become known to them when they were slaves in Egypt; and the relationship is again defined as an exclusive one, seeming to make room for no other deity. Other gods, however, are mentioned; as they were not in the *Shema*. But equally this time the words are more slippery than they seem. The Hebrew has 'before me', 'in front of me', not 'except me', a spatial description which seems to draw unnecessary attention to the presence of other deities. The second commandment, too, the one forbidding any plastic image to be used in representing God, is peculiar in its wording. The reason given for it is 'for I the Lord your God am a jealous God', which means, on the surface, jealous of such images, but must also refer to other gods, who habitually had images, and with whom Yahweh could be being confused.

These two confessional statements – that in the *Shema* and that in the first two commandments – are rather special. They show us orthodox and very subtle minds at work trying to encapsulate the essence of Israel's faith; yet they are unable to dispense with other gods. Or so it appears. But what should intrigue us about these passages is not the inability, but the reluctance of their formulators to dispense with comparison. They want to abase other gods but by no means to get rid of them; for that would not, in the polytheistic age in which they lived, serve their purposes. They know what they are about; they cannot but allow other gods some kind of real existence, for had these gods not thousands of devotees just across the border, and did not their worship often – too often – attract many Israelites? But they make sure that they contrast them with Yahweh to their permanent disadvantage.

Let us consider some descriptions of God that come, not from studied official prose, but from the freer world of poetry; and let us start, as we have done with prose, with Old Testament poetry at its seemingly most monotheistic, with Second Isaiah. This is the pseudonym of an unknown prophet in the period of the Babylonian exile, whose work survives in chapters 40–55 of the present biblical Book of Isaiah. He is usually credited with having attained at least as high a rating as the *Shema* on the monotheistic scale; and at first sight this seems to be the case. Take Isaiah 43.10 with its apparently carefully honed wording:

> 'You are my witnesses,' says the Lord,
>   'and my servant whom I have chosen,
> that you may know and believe me
>   and understand that I am He.
> Before me no god was formed,
>   nor shall there be any after me.'

This seems to state pretty plainly that no other gods except Yahweh have ever existed or shall exist. But we should hesitate before leaving it at that. There is also Isaiah 41.22–4 where Yahweh summons the gods of the nations to his presence and challenges them to produce their credentials.

> Tell us the former things, what they are,
>> that we may consider them,
> that we may know their outcome;
>> or declare to us the things to come.
> Tell us what is to come hereafter,
>> that we may know that you are gods;
> do good, or do harm,
>> that we may be dismayed and terrified.
> Behold, you are nothing,
>> and your work is naught.

The 'tell us' with its plural pronouns implies a meeting of the heavenly council to which these gods have to report and justify themselves. The picture is not unlike that in Psalm 82.1: 'God has taken his place in the divine council; in the midst of the gods he holds judgment'. There is no escaping the impression that for the prophet and his exiled audience in Isaiah 41.22ff. the other gods do very much exist. He is trying to revive the spirits of a downcast people who, if we only think for a moment of their situation, must have stood in genuine awe of the gods of their conquerors, and to convince them that their God, Yahweh, far from having been worsted by these gods, was more powerful than they were, and was about to intervene on behalf of his own people and lead them home to Zion. It is the exaggeration of faith that we hear in Isaiah 43.10, not a systematic theologian at work concerned to put his thoughts about God into the most appropriate conceptual terms. If we want to get near Second Isaiah's real state of mind on the issue that is before us, we should interpret the first passage in the light of the second, where the gods of the nations are tangibly there, in front of Yahweh, before he calls them 'nothing'. The many passages where Second Isaiah or other writers lampoon other gods as mere lumps of stone and precious metal should be understood in the same way (e.g. Isa. 46.1–7; Ps. 115.3–8).

With my next quotations the language of comparison comes clearly and robustly out into the open.

The victory song in Exodus 15 recounts the overthrow of Pharaoh's chariots in the waters, and then goes on (verse 11):

> Who is like thee, O Lord, among the gods?
> Who is like thee, majestic in holiness,
> terrible in glorious deeds, doing wonders?

Yahweh in this rather crude verse is but one among other gods; and the crudity is not mitigated if an emendation based on the Septuagint (Greek) translation, is accepted for the second line: 'majestic among the holy ones'. If this was the original text (and it is supported by the parallelism), the term 'gods' *could* be given the meaning 'angels', and the reference would be to the divine beings who surround Yahweh's throne in the heavenly council and who are not generally (despite Isa. 41.22ff. and Ps. 82) allowed to have any independence over against him. I am inclined to accept the emendation, but to argue on the contrary that in this verse 'gods' should be allowed to interpret 'holy ones'; for what would be the point if Yahweh were being contrasted with entities which were but picturesque extensions of himself?

Psalm 89.5–7 is even more extravagant in its wording:

> Let the heavens praise thy wonders, O Lord,
> thy faithfulness in the assembly of the holy ones!
> For who in the skies can be compared to the Lord?
> Who among the heavenly beings is like the Lord,
> a God feared in the council of the holy ones,
> great and terrible above all that are round about him?

These 'holy ones' and 'heavenly beings' (a weak rendering, for the Hebrew is literally 'sons of gods') are likewise members of Yahweh's court or council, and likewise they cannot be denuded of menace. It may by and large be true that when the Old Testament writers use the polytheistic terminology associated with this assembly, making Yahweh into the 'Lord of hosts' and 'a great King above all gods' (Ps. 95.3), it is their intention to enhance his majesty and holiness. Thus in Psalm 103.19–21 these gods become his 'angels', his 'hosts' and his 'ministers that do his will' and, as in Psalm 148.1–2, their chief task is to sing his praises. Thus former gods are recast, and Yahweh's council is made safe. But in Psalm 89, as in Exodus 15 (not to mention Isa. 41.22–4), there is still an unmistakable whiff of rivalry; the other divine beings are not simply playing a supporting role but have to be put in their place. It is as though they are being warned not to overreach themselves and reminded that, when it came to the crunch, they would not succeed. In Exodus 15, the implicit thought is that they could not have done what Yahweh had done in delivering his people from Egypt and harnessing wind and wave on their behalf. In Psalm 89 it is, in the immediately following verses, Yahweh's creation of the world that is the subject of celebration; and that too involved a battle and a victory, for cosmos did not emerge until chaos in the shape of a 'divine' monster called Rahab (in Ps. 74.12–17 it is called Leviathan) had been slain.

It may perhaps by now be evident why I devoted so much time earlier to arguing that a comparative dimension ought not to be removed from formulations like the *Shema*, however sedulously they may appear to us to avoid polytheism, and to countering today's too easy assumption that Second Isaiah's rhetoric is at basis monotheistic in our understanding of the term. The passages we examined first may steer clear of the lurid linguistic furniture of the passages we looked at next; but the message of the two sets of passages is essentially the same. Other gods are threateningly real in the problems they pose both for Yahweh and his people Israel; but he is King of heaven no less than of earth, and is as able to deal with other gods as he is to deal with their human counterparts like Egypt and Babylon; and that is why he alone is worthy of Israel's undivided allegiance. The desire to contrast Yahweh with other gods so that he may be seen to be incomparably superior to them is endemic in Old Testament religious language in all its stages, and it is wrong of modern scholars to want it to disappear with the passage of time. As long as we do not grasp that fundamental point and insist on fitting ancient Israel's religion into an evolutionary scheme based on a movement from polytheism through henotheism towards monotheism, we shall miss what makes it tick. It is the incomparability of its God, a notion that can only be got across by using the vocabulary of comparison with other gods, who cannot do what its God does.

Some of the language about God used in the Old Testament, as the above two incursions into it show, is hardly acceptable today. But that is hardly the point. The effectiveness of such language in its ancient context cannot be denied, and that is what is important for this book. We shall in the pages that follow (see especially Chapter 6) be examining a good few of the Old Testament images of God. The strangeness and unfamiliarity of them will constantly be before us, but our objections, be they of taste or disbelief, are in the last resort irrelevant. We are asked to understand the Scriptures, not to approve of them.

THE RHETORIC OF

HEBREW PROSE WRITING

IN THE LONG prose first half of the Old Testament there is
chronicle writing and there are lists of names and legal and
religious codes and accounts of the divisions of the land or of
the building of the Jerusalem temple; but these are not literary
texts. Apart from a few old poems preserved here and there
among the prose records, for example the Song of Deborah in
Judges 5, and the Book of Deuteronomy which though in prose,
purports to be an address of Moses to the people on the borders
of the Promised Land and contains therefore, apart from legal
material, a lot of figurative language and rhetorical techniques
(cf. chs. 6–8, 28–30), only the stories in prose reveal much sign
of the kind of literary features we are looking for.

These stories are very varied, ranging from the origin stories
(or, as some would have it, myths) of the early chapters of
Genesis and the heroic legends that revolve round Abraham
and the other patriarchs in the later chapters of Genesis through
the epic accounts of the escape from Egypt, the wilderness
wandering, and the settlement of Canaan in the Books of
Exodus to Joshua, to the tales of heroes like Gideon and
Samson and particularly Saul and David in the Books of
Judges and Samuel, to what we might call stories of the
saints like those of Elijah and Elisha in the Books of Kings,
and to the memoirs of Ezra and Nehemiah in the books given
these names. To be included with them, but occupying small
books scattered here and there, are several individual short
stories like the pastoral romance of Ruth, the courtly romance
of Esther, the parable of Jonah, the diaspora adventures of
Daniel, or the old folk-tale of Job (chs. 1–2, 42) on which that
book is based, all likewise in prose. Most of these stories are so
arranged that they follow a rough historical progression, but
the telling of history is not their chief purpose. Rather they are
in Scripture to remind later ages of the heroic figures of their

nation and religion, to instil in them faith and pride and not a little caution, to provide exemplars of good living and bad, to help them celebrate their God, who had been worshipped by these forefathers and who, they believed, had given them the law and the temple and the other institutions, the foundations of which are also lovingly recorded in their Scriptures and to which the stories supply, as it were, a human background. The earlier of the stories make us think of Homer and other ancient bards, and the later of Sir Walter Scott and his historical novels; and there is no reason why we should not think of Homer or Scott. The stories were more than epics and tales of the past to those who included them in Holy Writ, but they were at least that; and those who heard or read them must have appreciated them as imaginative stories, as we still do, even if sometimes we are a bit uncomfortable about it, remembering where they come from.

What then are the characteristic marks of the biblical stories and the characteristic strategies used by their composers? The marks and strategies may not appear in every story, but they appear sufficiently frequently to impart a certain atmosphere to the genre. I will take most of my examples from the story of Joseph and his brothers in Genesis chapters 37ff., but I will cite examples from other stories if they seem more appropriate.

Why prose?

It should, firstly, surprise us more than it does that the stories are all in prose; for their counterparts in other cultures at the same period are in poetry, like the two great works of Homer or, from nearer home, the long creation myth (Enuma Elish) or the epic tale of Gilgamesh from Mesopotamia, or the myths and legends from Ugarit (Ras Shamra) in Syria. Like the Greeks of the time of Herodotus, who began in that civilization the art of historiography, the writers of the Hebrew Bible seem to have found out a little earlier that prose was a more congenial and adaptable medium for writing about the past than the old poetry of their race with its fixed conventions. We do not know whether there was in old Israel an original national epic in poetry covering much the same subjects as the early books of the Old Testament, and sung at the various festivals and maybe even at gatherings in the villages by professional bards or singers of tales. I like to think that there was, for how otherwise were the old traditions handed down in the long tribal period before, from monarchical times on, they were given a permanent shape – and in prose – in the nascent documents which eventually crystallized into Scripture? Nothing has survived, and we have to look at the relatively rare songs and psalms which celebrate historical events or contain quite extensive pieces of narrative which have been preserved in, for example, Exodus 15 (The Song of Moses), Judges 5 (The Song of Deborah – compare the prose version in Judg. 4), or in Psalms 78, 105 and so on, to get some idea of what such an epic corpus might have sounded like.

But why was only narrative affected by this change to prose? Most of the other genres in the Hebrew Bible – prophetic oracles, psalms for worship, wisdom collections like Proverbs, even tough theological disputations or semi-dramas like the Book of Job – are in poetry as in neighbouring cultures (Ecclesiastes is an exception, being mainly in prose, but it is rather late). Was the old epic poetry style, which the biblical writers knew from their environment, if not from their own literary history, too stultifying for tales in which their God played a role, was it felt to be too tied to polytheism with its constant search for archetypes and its lack of interest in the progress of events? Had in other words ancient Israel's unique religion with its single deity and its concern for the working out of his purposes in history, something to do with it? Or was it simply that Israel's writers discovered a bit before the Greeks that prose suited better than poetry the tracing of the complicated interplay of event and character, of 'fate' and endeavour, that is involved in human affairs?

I suspect that both reasons may have had a part to play. But however it came about, prose not poetry was used for history writing and, the same thing really at this time, for the kind of story-writing that we find everywhere in the Hebrew Old Testament. Historicized fiction or fictionalized history is what we are really talking about. We can be reasonably confident that the events or something like them happened, but the writers were more concerned with the effect that they had on the people of their time, and they used all the resources of their writing craft to induce that effect, to get the people thinking about the past and its influence on the present, above all, to stretch their imaginations on how their God had disposed himself in their previous history and, by extrapolation, on what he might yet have in store for them.

Composite authorship

It comes as a shock to those of this age used to individual authorship and modern publishing ways to realize that the Old Testament, especially in its prose parts, is a combined enterprise. Nor is it the outcome of editorial and assembling activity only, but of something more thoroughgoing. In the prophetic corpus we can perhaps speak mainly of editors who gathered together and arranged the surviving oracles of individual prophets. This is not so with the stories, which began probably as oral tradition (the earlier of them anyway), and passed through several stages as accounts of laws and institutions were incorporated and the change from poetry to prose took place, before ending up as something like the Old Testament as we now know it. It was a vast growth, beginning as soon as there was an identifiable people to be addressed, and continuing for several centuries, the literary part in the amalgam being recognized, not by an author's name, but only by its genre. Many hands were at work in this long process, and no one was kept back by matters of protocol or copyright. In the case of the Pentateuch (or at any rate its first four books: Genesis, Exodus, Leviticus, Numbers) three documentary sources have been recognized by modern scholarship, one called J for Yahwistic (using the divine name Yahweh, in German *Jahve*, translated in English by 'The Lord'), one called E for Elohistic (using the divine name Elohim, translated into English by 'God'), and one called P for 'priestly' thought to be the latest of the three (in German *Priesterschrift*, using both divine names). A fourth document or school of tradents (transmitters of tradition), called D for Deuteronomy, was responsible for the Pentateuchal book of that name, and as 'Deuteronomist', for the editing and, in many places, the writing of the books from Joshua to Kings. A group of tradents, related to P, was responsible for Chronicles and for Ezra and Nehemiah. One of these four or five group or other editors or redactors no doubt preserved the smaller writings like Ruth or Esther in much the same way.

The search by scholars for sources and redactors has thus been intense, but it has probably been overdone. Before the rise of modern biblical scholarship, no one seems to have been particularly interested in sources and growth, but almost automatically thought in terms of single authors like Moses for the Pentateuch, David for the Psalms, or Solomon for the Wisdom literature. We cannot go back now to that time, and should be grateful to the scholars for recovering the complicated route by which the Old Testament reached us. But there is a down-side too; excavatory scholarship in the last resort is theory, not fact, and we must deplore the fissiparous tendencies of its practitioners. We can admit the excellent work they have done in substituting the more satisfactory notions of growth and variety for the previous timeless reading, too often encrusted with dogma. But at the same time we should think more often than they did of the final result of their endeavours, which is the Old Testament as we have it, and study more closely the considerable skill with which everything has been put together to make a meaningful whole.

Thus the order of creation in Genesis 1, which is P, differs from that in Genesis 2.4–7, which is J and E together (the divine name is 'The Lord God') and in which man was created before the plants. The redactors who followed the one passage with the other must have been aware of this discrepancy, but they were also aware that there was a reason for the second passage. It is expressly stated in 2.5 that there was no rain so that plants could grow, but only underground water (AV 'mist') which could support trees; this was because there were shortly to be trees in Eden, whereas plants ('thorns and thistles') came later as a result of Adam's disobedience (3.18). The few verses in Genesis 2.4–7 were not then an alternative to chapter 1 but were setting the scene for what happened in the Garden of Eden story, and for that reason the redactors ignored the contradictions and retained the verses; they knew what they were doing.

The Joseph stories are rather different, however, a long combined narrative rather than two short narratives set side by side and, though they were apparently derived from a separate J and E, there are few discrepancies visible in the combined work, and those that survive have been skilfully circumvented, so that we hardly notice that they are there.

One is the confusion in Genesis chapter 37 between the Midianites and the Ishmaelites (see verses 25ff.). The brothers saw a caravan of Ishmaelites passing by and conceived a plan to sell Joseph, whom they had cast into a pit, to them. But meanwhile, a second caravan, this time of Midianites, came along, and they lifted Joseph out of the pit, and sold him to the Ishmaelites, all unknown to the brothers, and the Ishmaelites took him down into Egypt; and Simeon when he visited the pit on his own (having the idea of rescuing him and delivering him back to his father) found him missing. He told the other brothers, and it was then they concocted the plan involving the coat of many colours. However, at the end of the chapter (verse 36) it is the Midianites who sold him when they got to Egypt, yet in 39.1, in a recap, Potiphar buys him from the Ishmaelites.

Because of this stutter, many scholars assume that we are dealing with two divergent versions of essentially the same traditional story belonging to different documentary sources, one in which the brothers do indeed sell him to the Midianites and there are no Ishmaelites on the scene, and one in which no Midianites appear but a caravan of Ishmaelites rescues him from a pit. It is a plausible theory, which may very well be right. The reference to the Midianites taking him down to Egypt comes from one version and suits as well the combined story, whereas the reference to Ishmaelites in 39.1 comes from the other version and was retained in the combined story by an oversight. But the matter cannot be allowed to rest there. Some comment is required on the combined version being more complicated than either of the single versions and therefore representing more fittingly the state of mind the brothers would have been in on discovering that their younger brother had so nicely delivered himself into their hands, and their consequent rather frantic scheming to get rid of him. On any reckoning the combined story is a better one than either of the single ones with only one passing caravan and, in spite of one small error, it reflects great credit on those who did the combining.

Another place in the Joseph story where the scholars find traces of two documents is where the brothers are dumbfounded when they open their sacks at a staging post, on their first return from Egypt, and find their money in them (Gen. 42.27–8). It is a dramatic moment, but it is stretching our credulity more than a little to find that they were likewise dumbfounded on finding the money after they had returned to Canaan (42.35). The words in which this incident is told are uncannily similar to the words used of the brothers on the earlier occasion. It does look as though the drama of discovery is being related twice, and that originally each of the source documents had only related it once, but placed it at different points in the story. But as in the case of the Midianites–Ishmaelites stutter in chapter 37, it hardly seems to matter. We could even surmise that it was Jacob alone who was surprised on the second occasion, the brothers feigning surprise in order to avoid embarrassment; and it is quite likely that the redactor who combined the two original accounts wished his audience's thoughts to go in that direction. Again the combined story is better than either of the original ones, considerably increasing the tension and highlighting the brothers' duplicity.

To sum up: we are obliged to notice that many of the biblical stories were not composed by one author and that what we have now is a combined job. But it is by no means a botched job; it is the result of considerable artistry. The cracks may show but they are never allowed to obtrude, and the skill of any previous writers is retained and if anything added to. This is a more profound observation than the simple one that the writers used sources in the first place. It is what they made of these sources that matters. We owe the redactors who worked on the sources a lot; they enhance rather than diminish our appreciation of the stories.

Reticence

One of the most remarkable features of Hebrew narrative is its essential reticence, which sometimes spills over into frugality. This is something of a conundrum, when one thinks of it; for the Bible is supposed to be didactic, getting its message over pretty obviously, and this is often true of many of the prophets, for instance, or the Book of Proverbs. But the stories proceed in a different manner.

Take the setting of the scene in the story of Joseph in Genesis 37.2–4:

Joseph, being seventeen years old, was shepherding the flock with his brothers; he was a lad with the sons of Bilhah and

Zilpah, his father's wives; and Joseph brought an ill report of them to their father. Now Israel loved Joseph more than any other of his children, because he was the son of his old age; and he made him a long robe with sleeves. But when his brothers saw that their father loved him more than all his brothers, they hated him, and could not speak peaceably to him.

No dates are mentioned and no places, there is no description of scene or person, none of that paraphernalia of circumstantial detail that not only modern historians but modern novelists feel obliged to give their readers. Thomas Mann, for instance, in his Joseph novel has a whole chapter on the 'coat of many colours' (AV), how it was obtained and where, what it looked like, and the electric effect when Joseph first marched out wearing it. The RSV with its 'long robe with sleeves' is more accurate than the AV, though it dispenses with a magical phrase in the English. The Hebrew term, probably a trade name describing a particular kind of garment, occurs only once elsewhere, in 2 Samuel 13.18, describing something worn by a princess, associated therefore with the moneyed and leisured classes. Joseph clearly was being let off his stint on the farm by an over-indulgent father. The detail, by being specially mentioned, is important and not merely evocative. The only other detail of this kind in the passage is the description of Joseph as the 'son of his (Jacob's) old age'. He was nothing of the sort; Benjamin should on this score have been his favourite. Was Benjamin also being ignored by Jacob at this time, only becoming of concern to him later when Joseph, he thought, was no more? This sort of detail is cryptic, explaining Joseph's favouritism but raising at the same time questions in our minds. Not only is the passage devoid on the whole of circumstantial detail but those details which are mentioned are as likely as not to prove elusive.

That we are confronted here with a powerful narrative style should be recognized more in our commentaries than it is. An even better example is provided by the near sacrifice of Isaac in Genesis 22, or the 'binding' of Isaac, as it is termed in Jewish tradition. There is again no description of the location beyond a statement that it was a mountain in a district called Moriah three days' journey from Beersheba – though in 2 Chronicles 3.1

Moriah is connected with the Jerusalem temple, and that may
have been the point of the reference, that Isaac's ordeal took
place in what was later to be Israel's capital. Nor is there any
description of what Abraham and Isaac looked like, of the
clothes they wore, of what the weather was like, of what kind of
rite was envisaged or what its purpose may have been. God
gives no reason for his command, but simply issues it. We are
told nothing of Abraham's reaction, of his amazement, his
anger perhaps, his bitterness, his grief; and only one small
question – where is the animal? – gives us a hint of Isaac's
bewilderment at what is going on. Likewise, after it is all over
and the ram has been slaughtered instead of Isaac, there are no
tears of relief and joy, no words even exchanged between father
and son. We get only a renewal of the promise in the usual
conventional (and creating a foil with the rest of the story,
rather lengthy) words, and an announcement that the party
returned to Beersheba. It seems almost as if the writer is trying
his best to empty his story of drama. Yet how dramatic it is!
How strongly God's imperial claims come across! How vivid is
the progress of father and son through the empty landscape!
How unbearable is the suspense as Isaac asks his question!
What echoes resound in Abraham's answer, 'God will provide
himself the lamb'! How taut is the tension as Abraham raises
his knife, how immense the relief when he catches sight of a
ram caught in a bush! How unutterably savage too are God's
words at the end – 'your only son' – as if Ishmael didn't even
exist. This is Hebrew story-telling at its masterly best. It is not at
all the kind of story-telling we are used to from modern novels.

It is not even the kind of story-telling that most ancient
peoples were used to. This fundamental feature of Hebrew
narrative style is contrasted with the equally epic or heroic and
equally ancient style of Homer by Eric Auerbach in the celebrated first chapter of his book *Mimesis: The Representation of
Reality in Western Literature* (Princeton University Press 1946),
entitled 'Odysseus' scar'. The chapter takes its title from the
famous recognition scene in Book 19 of the Odyssey. Odysseus
has come home from his long travels, and is in disguise, but his
old housekeeper recognizes him by the scar on his thigh as she
washes his feet. In surprise she drops his feet into the basin. It is
an intensely dramatic moment, yet in between the act of
recognition and the act of dropping the foot – what a place to

choose! – there is a lengthy digression giving the whole story of how Odysseus had received the scar from a boar's tusk many years before. How characteristic all this is of Homer's style! We feel the drama, yet we are willing to digress with him and get lost with him in the story of the scar, and we are equally willing to return with him to the main scene when he is ready. There is no unbearable tension, no desire to 'turn the pages'; we realize that we must travel at Homer's pace, stopping every now and again for fulsome descriptions of places and people, of dress or armour, of things eaten or drunk, for long speeches in which the characters explain in great detail what they have done or are going to do and why or, as in this passage, for lengthy digressions to other times and scenes and actions.

Occasionally in the biblical stories we meet with some of these conventions – as in the panelled repetitions of Genesis 1, or the slow pace of Genesis 24 (the finding of a wife for Isaac), or the emotionally charged speech of Judah in Genesis 44. This is only to be expected, since both the Greek and the Hebraic stories have to work within the broad parameters of what is, or at any rate started as, folk literature. But even in these biblical parallels there is nothing so replete as in Homer; and Genesis 22 or the beginning of Genesis 37, where the old conventions have been pared down to a minimum, are much more representative. There is no way that the Old Testament asks us to surrender to time-consuming explanations and descriptions as Homer does, so that we hardly need to make a single query or wonder about a single particular. Rather, we have to make inferences all the while. Indeed, the contrast of styles within what is essentially the same genre of epic or heroic narrative is so wide that the biblical critics should be emphasizing it at every possible juncture. That instead they fill their commentaries with arguments about documents and sources and historicity only shows their small sense of priorities.

In assessing the influence of the biblical stories Auerbach speaks of them being 'fraught with background' over against the Homeric stories where all is foreground. It is a happy phrase and must have something to do with the God whose presence haunts them, though Auerbach rather avoids theological talk. Robert Alter in his book *The Art of Biblical Narrative* (George Allen and Unwin 1981) waxes a little more theologically, speaking about ancient Israel's exposure to the concept of monotheism. He does not say so in so many words, but it is as though the story-teller is forced to make room for God, and the way he chooses is the way of reticence. He realizes that he is in a real sense speaking for God, and he says as little as possible in case he be accused of taking God's place. God's majesty, freedom, jealousy, transcendence, and grace are marvellously safeguarded. Men and women are not allowed to think too highly of themselves – there are no humanistic ideals in these stories – but they too are allowed to retain their freedom and their individuality. What was it like to be a human being living out one's days in such a society as ancient Israel's where such a God held sway? That is the question to which the story-tellers of the Old Testament addressed themselves, and they answered it with humility and with a dash of irony even but never with too much assurance.

Key words and resonances

The repetition of key words in a text serves various purposes. It may ease genre-recognition, as the same words or phrases recur again and again in the same kind of writing, as in formulae of blessing or cursing or promise or as in psalms of praise or lament; they may be almost accidental and lead the reader to connect passages which were originally separate; or they may have an almost structural or thematic role within a single text or a group of related texts, carrying a heavy significance for the meaning of the whole. I prefer to call such repeated words echoes or resonances, because in a literature like the Bible readers often find them across the whole Old Testament, and Christians not infrequently use them, legitimately or not, to illuminate the New Testament through the Old.

In the Joseph stories the word 'brother' is worth investigating for the large number of twists and nuances it carries in different contexts. The words 'remember' and 'forget' in Genesis 40.23; 41.9; 42.9 and Genesis 41.51 have a longer perspective, reminding us not only of a forgetful chief butler and a Joseph who forgot his past but, looking back, of texts like Genesis 8.1 ('But God remembered Noah') and, looking forward, of texts like Psalm 137.1 ('By the waters of Babylon, there we sat down and wept, when we remembered Zion') and Isaiah 49.15 ('Even these may forget, yet I will not forget you'); unlike human beings God does not forget (though compare the lamentation psalm, Ps. 13.1 'How long, O Lord? Wilt thou forget me for ever?'). The word 'honest' (Gen. 42.11) is in context heavily ironic considering the lies the brothers had already told Jacob, and would do so again. The word 'dungeon' used in Genesis 40.15 by Joseph to describe his Egyptian prison should be translated 'pit', for it is the same Hebrew word as is used of the pit into which his brothers cast him in Genesis 37.22–4; no English version I have on my shelves has caught this resonance, not even the AV, which is on the whole more faithful than the others in rendering Hebrew words by the same English equivalent. The word 'silver', usually translated 'money', for example, in the incidents involving the finding of the brothers' money in the mouth of their sacks, occurs more than twenty times in the Joseph stories. It is fortunate that in Genesis 37.28 we have 'twenty shekels of silver' (the price the Midianites sold Joseph to the Ishmaelites for) and can trace the resonances back to Abraham buying the field of Machpelah (Gen. 23.13–16) and forward to the atonement money of Exodus 30.16 or the redemption money of Numbers 3.48 or, if we are Christians, to the thirty pieces of silver which figure in the Passion story.

But the key word above all in the Joseph narratives is 'know', with which we might include cognates from the same Hebrew root like 'recognize' or 'show'. Here is a list of the more significant references in Genesis chapters 39–45:

he (Potiphar) has no concern (lit. does not know). (39.8)

Since God has shown you (lit. made you to know) all this, there is none so discreet ... (of the appointment of Joseph as vizier) (41.39)

Joseph ... knew them, but he treated them like strangers ... (there is a play on the Hebrew verbs here). Thus Joseph knew his brothers, but they did not know him. (42.7–8)

They did not know that Joseph understood them. (42.23)

By this I shall know that you are honest men (i.e. when you bring Benjamin). (42.33)

Could we in any way know that he would say, 'Bring your brother down'? (43.7)

We do not know who put our money in our sacks (the

steward, an Egyptian, tells them it must have been their God). (43.22)

Do you not know that such a man as I can indeed divine? (44.15)

Joseph made himself known to his brothers. (45.1)

Notice first how Joseph knows and seems to be in charge: he knows who his brothers are, he knows how to practice divination, he even makes himself known to his brothers. But in reality he does not know all that much until the end when he suddenly realizes what it has all been about. In that sense he is as ignorant as the brothers, whose lack of knowledge and whose frustration and bewilderment are rubbed in both savagely and poignantly. They are all in reality as ignorant as Potiphar who in chapter 39 knows or cares for nothing but the food he eats. How ironic that the one hint about the only one who really knew is given by an Egyptian ('God must have put treasure in your sacks'). Listen to these reverberating 'knows' and we have a beautiful picture of a man who knows a lot about his life and destiny when in fact he knows very little. Taken together with the scant but extremely significant references in this story, we are being prepared, almost surreptitiously, for the story's last and most dramatic scene when all of a sudden it comes home to Joseph, to the brothers, and to us in the audience who, above, behind, and below the pathetic posturings of knowledgeable humanity, is alone in charge of the movement of events.

The word 'know' plays a similar role in the Book of Job which can only be described as theological; Job and his friends know, confidentally and abrasively, what God is up to for both good and ill – they are after all the representatives of Wisdom, the philosophy of their age – but both have to be taught hard lessons when God at last speaks for himself (consult a concordance and trace the word through the book, and you will see). The repeated or key word resonates meaningfully throughout not only the prose tales of Scripture but the poetic pieces as well, and should be diligently sought.

Characterization

Character in the Old Testament is as much indicated by what
the characters say as by what they do or what happens to them,
which is in the stories on the whole so fleetingly etched, and in
poetic pieces often not told at all. The characters in the stories
can talk at some length and seem sometimes to be as voluble as
the story-teller in his narrative portions is laconic; there is thus
a contrast of style within some stories, that of Joseph being no
exception – between the narrator speaking for himself and
exasperating us with his terseness and the words which he
puts in his characters' mouths which on occasion exasperate us
by their verbosity. One reason for this is that Semitic speech is,
especially in formal conversation or utterances, repetitive and
extravagant (see the bargaining scene between Abraham and
Ephron the Hittite in Gen. 23 which leads up to the purchase of
a burying place for Sarah in Hebron).

But Semitic speech, as again in Genesis 23, can also be
evasive; it both reveals and hides human motives, and in
exploring this the Hebrew story-tellers are masters. There is a
fascination with conversation and speechifying which is almost
modern when one considers the amount of talk in a typical
novel today. But I do not want to press that comparison too far.
What I want to stress is that, though we sometimes learn a lot,
we do not always get the kind of information we want, and we
have to do almost as much inferring from what the characters
say as from the laconic narrative stretches. At any rate we do
not have, in quite a few of the conversations and speeches,
characters dispensing information from on high, as we not
uncommonly do in, for instance, the sermons of the prophets.
Thus in the Joseph tale we have confident men and fearful men,
but both are seen in the end to be as helpless and ignorant in
the face of life's vicissitudes as we are in our day.

Thus we have Joseph arrogant and boastful at the start of
Genesis chapter 37, then falling silent at the end (suffering in
silence?); we have him saying all the right things in chapters
39–41 as he deals with Potiphar and his wife, with the two
prominent prisoners, and not least with Pharaoh – yet one or
two remarks, notably in 41.51 when Manasseh is named, show
that the mask can slip and the rememberer forget; and in
chapters 42–5 he first has us on his side and then outrageously

47

overdoes it, he plays with fire in his scheming – yet he can also weep. Where in all this is the real Joseph; or is it all the real Joseph, endearing and suspicious reactions both, warts and all? And we have the brothers, full of hatred at the beginning, telling lies and dispensing cruelty, yet after they have had a deserved come-uppance, we begin to sympathize with them in their bewilderment and despair as they say (42.28), 'What is this that God has done to us?', where God is probably equivalent to not much more than our 'fate'. However, just before that, searching around for an explanation, they had wondered, with the irony of a bad conscience, whether it might not be a reckoning for Joseph's blood (42.21–2); yet on their second visit they are back with God equals 'fate' as Judah says (44.16), of the discovery of the cup, 'What shall we say to my lord?' 'God has found out the guilt of your servants', the one phrase meaning more or less the same as the other – they didn't think that they had been guilty of anything, but are perfectly well aware that there is nothing they can do about it. Are these men learning the lessons of life, or are they so far gone in fear as simply to feel helpless?

But again, we cannot avoid noticing how it is Reuben and Judah, the ones who had taken the lead in despatching Joseph in chapter 37 who are the most solicitous later on behalf of Benjamin. Reuben offers his two sons as hostages at the end of chapter 42, and Judah is the one who stands up to Joseph with his long and remarkable speech in the second half of chapter 44. It is a beautiful example of Hebrew rhetoric at its best. Judah is neither obsequious nor defiant. He accepts that the great man in front of him had spoken both justly and graciously in condemning Benjamin and letting the rest of them return. But back in Canaan he had solemnly promised their father to bring Benjamin home unharmed, and he had no recourse but to try a last gambit on his behalf. He asks that he himself instead of Benjamin should bear the punishment of slavery. It is a noble offer, nobly made, which surely cancels out the shame and meanness of what he had done to Joseph those many years before – not to mention what he had done to Tamar before that (chapter 38).

And as he makes it, he gives a description, charged with emotion, of an ageing father doting on Benjamin because his elder brother was dead, afraid even to let him out of his sight;

of ten harassed brothers, not knowing what to do as disaster after disaster overtakes them; of the Egyptian official before him whose insistent questioning it was that had set the whole sorry series of events in motion; and again, at the close, of the old man in Canaan turning his face to the wall in inconsolable grief and giving up life's struggle. It is a speech that would draw blood from a stone, and it worked its immediate power on Joseph; yet it is full of delicious ironies which Judah cannot have intended, and it does not mention God once. How are we to judge it, and how judge Judah?

Finally, there is old Jacob, the supreme rhetorician of grief, the one who had in his youth schemed to steal his brother's blessing, deceiving an old man as he was now, daring even at Peniel to fight God's angel and wrest from him the same blessing, apprehensive and calculating as he met with Esau while Esau, the man who had once despised the blessing, runs to meet and forgive him; and now, like Peter in Jesus' prophecy of *his* old age (John 21.18–19), being told to do what he did not want to do, reacting helplessly to events, and uttering a veritable cascade of doom-laden verses: 'You would bring down my grey hairs with sorrow to Sheol' (Gen. 42.38), 'If it must be so ...' (43.11), 'If I am bereaved of my children, I am bereaved' (43.14). But when at the end, after years of sadness and, we must hope, recrimination and conscience-searching, when he saw the wagons that Joseph had sent to fetch him, 'the spirit of their father Jacob revived; and Israel said, "It is enough; Joseph my son is still alive; I will go and see him before I die"' (45.28). Even for the most inveterate of misanthropes, old age in miniature, Israel in miniature, perhaps humankind in miniature, there is a happy ending.

The activity of God

God appears in the Hebrew stories in a plethora of guises. The Book of Genesis covers most of these. Sometimes God appears himself or in the shape of an angel, speaking directly to human beings, sometimes he is spoken to by the characters, and on other occasions spoken of by them as they react to his presence, or by the writer as he discusses what his presence might mean.

The crucial verses in the Joseph epic in this regard are the ones which Joseph addresses to his brothers after telling them who he is: at 45.5ff. he reassures them, '... do not be distressed, or angry with yourselves, because you sold me here; for God sent me before you to preserve ... for you a remnant on earth ... So it was not you who sent me here, but God', and later at 50.19–20, when after Jacob's death the brothers are naturally apprehensive again about how he will treat them, he says, 'Fear not, for am I in the place of God? As for you, you meant evil against me; but God meant it for good, to bring it about that many people should be kept alive, as they are today.'

These two little speeches express in the colourful language of story the essence of what the theologians in their more technical language call the doctrine of providence. Under this heading are grouped some of the knottiest problems of theology. How does God govern and maintain the universe he created? How does his activity relate to the laws of nature, the forces of history, the freedom of the individual? What is the connection between his general providence over the universe and what may be called his special providence in the life of his own worshippers? Under what circumstances does God, as it were, break his own rules and work a miracle? Most troublesome of all, where is there a place for evil, especially in its most tragic manifestations, within the idea of a loving and caring providence?

The two statements of Joseph home in on what to the believer must be the central core of any such doctrine, namely that God is able so to organize the world as to bring good out of evil. They express in their own way the conviction of Paul of Tarsus (Rom. 8.28), 'We know that in everything God works for good with those who love him'. Notice the prominent 'We know', the great key word of the Joseph epic; but what Paul is talking about, and Joseph (though the word 'know' does not actually occur in the two relevant passages), is the knowledge that comes with looking back, in Joseph's case the new knowledge to replace that which he had previously claimed.

There is no doubt that the way Joseph speaks about God's activity in these two passages is more congenial to us today than the way that activity is set forth in other passages of Scripture, notably the earlier part of Genesis. The tales of Abraham and Jacob think on the whole in terms of God interfering in and with the normal, appearing out of the blue as it were and compelling Abraham to leave his former homeland, challenging him to believe that a child could be born to Sarah when she was long past child-bearing age, calling upon him to sacrifice his only son (!) to him, leaving Ishmael out in the cold and giving his partisan blessing to Isaac. It is the same in the Jacob saga, as he lets Jacob steal birthright and blessing and then appears to him at Bethel to assure him of his protection, or as he ignores Jacob's life of deceit in Mesopotamia to fight with him finally at Peniel – only to let him win. These stories are particularly interested in God's 'special' providence, and other peoples are hardly mentioned (despite the initial promise to Abraham in Gen. 12.1–3) except as they impinge, for the most part hostilely and therefore to be repulsed, on the life of his chosen people. The God of these stories is expected to appear and disappear suddenly, to perform miracles, to issue life or death challenges, to be experienced in the unusual and the abnormal.

The Joseph epic, on the other hand, tries to take a more comprehensive and subtler view of divine providence. It invites us to think of God working behind the scenes, controlling but not forcing the pace of events, permitting things to happen rather than directly causing them to happen, achieving his ends *through* men's actions rather than in spite of them. Thus he does not send the famine, as he did fire and brimstone on Sodom and Gomorrah; it simply comes. And at the end, it is not only Jacob's small clan that are delivered, though it is they who are meant by the word 'remnant' in 45.7. 'All the earth' (41.57) comes to Egypt to buy grain, including presumably Jacob's Canaanite neighbours, who are so roundly condemned in other parts of Scripture, and presumably everyone else who came was also preserved alive.

All this is so like the quiet and considered way so many of us today arrive at the assurance that God and not any other force, human or mechanical, is in charge of our lives, and indeed in charge of the lives of those around us, be they believers or not, that we are bound to be warmed and encouraged by it. We look back over our lives and we *know* that it is so. We do not, most of us, experience those shattering confrontations with the divine that people like Abraham or Jacob seem always to be experiencing, and which some in the clerical profession are always telling us is the only way to be saved. Our experience is much more like Joseph's and his brothers, a realization every now and again that events we once thought had no purpose in them, events that perhaps were calamitous in their immediate consequences, events even in which we ourselves acted meanly, were in fact blessings in disguise, part and parcel of a larger, and ongoing, divine plan for us and ours. It is in the last resort that realization, never continuous, always partial, but none the less real, that enables us to grit our teeth in hope and press forward in the battle of life. As old Jacob said (45.28), 'It is enough'.

And that will do for the literary side of prose writing in the Old Testament and the rhetoric it embodies. Reticence and reserve, key words and resonances, characterization through direct speech – these are the tools of the Hebrew story-teller's trade, and how skilfully they are deployed in the story of Joseph, on which I have concentrated, and in their own way in the other biblical stories which I have not or hardly mentioned. Of course, theology is involved in the stories too, but it is theology in narrative disguise. The activity of God is explored in all its facets in a non-technical fashion, and that has had to be looked at too, if only to make it clear that the toughest theology is not necessarily found in the work of the professionals, but can come to us in gentler and more imaginative ways.

−4−

THE RHETORIC AND
MELODIES OF HEBREW POETRY

POETRY IS EMPLOYED for most literary purposes in the Old
Testament with the exception of narrative which, for
reasons suggested in the last chapter, uses prose. The three
main kinds are prophetic (or oracular) poetry, psalms (or lyric)
poetry, and wisdom (or didactic) poetry. Within each of these
kinds both positive and negative notes are struck: of judgement
and comfort in the Prophets, of praise and lament in the
Psalms, and of the traditional and the questioning in wisdom.
I shall follow these contrasting notes or melodies in this attempt
to assess the spirit and effectiveness of biblical poetic rhetoric.
But first something needs to be said about the mechanics of
poetry in the Old Testament and how it is distinguished from
prose.

The shape of Hebrew poetry

Poetry is differentiated from prose in biblical Hebrew by two
formal features: first, a rough metre based on a certain number
of stresses in a line and second, parallelism of content between
adjacent lines.

We can take an English prose sentence and without great
difficulty put in the main stresses:

> He wróte his expériences in a díary évery dáy

It is the same in Hebrew; a native speaker ignores small words
like the definite article (there is no indefinite article in Hebrew),
prepositions, conjunctions and so forth and stressless syllables
within a word, and homes in on those syllables which saying
the sentence aloud tells him are the prominent ones. Thus the
first sentence in Genesis can be marked:

> *bereshíth bará elohím eth-hashshamáyim we eth-haárets*

It contains five stresses just like the English sentence quoted above, and indeed like the same verse in English translation:

In the begínning Gód créated the héavens and the eárth

It will often happen that the number of stresses is broadly similar in equivalent sentences in the two languages, though in Hebrew words the stress is always on the last or the penultimate syllable, whereas in English it tends to land on the first syllable or one near it; and a prose sentence in Hebrew, as in English, can theoretically be of any length. As far as poetry is concerned, however, the lines are restricted in length, but whereas English metre usually deals in complicated patterns of stressed and unstressed syllables, Hebrew metre deals with the stresses alone, differing only from prose in the number that are permitted. Easily the commonest metre is three stresses in the line, but if the emotion is strong, there may be only two, while if the mood is meditative, there may be four or even five.

But that feature in itself would simply mean that Hebrew poetry lacked the elasticity of Hebrew prose and had a stilted ring to it. To get the full flavour of Hebrew poetry, a second feature has to be taken into account, namely *parallelism* of the wording (and the meaning) between one line and the next. This makes the basic unit not the line but the couplet, a pair of lines in which the second line says much the same as the first.

But let us listen to some examples. Proverbs 3.13–17 exhibits the normal 3+3 metre (in Hebrew, of course):

13. Happy is the man who finds wisdom,
    and the man who gets understanding,
14. for the gain from it is better than gain from silver
    and its profit better than gold.
15. She is more precious than jewels,
    and nothing you desire can compare with her.
16. Long life is in her right hand;
    in her left are riches and honour.
17. Her ways are ways of pleasantness,
    and all her paths are peace.

Stilted it may seem on a first hearing, but on the whole monotony is avoided by the small variations that may occur in the second line of a couplet. Thus in verse 13 'Happy is the man' is literally 'the happinesses of the man', which has here one stress, though it could have two (it is an instance of the construct state, as it is called, which links closely together two nouns in a genitive relationship, English commonly rendering it by using the preposition 'of'); in the second line this phrase is answered by 'the man', the first part of the construct state being understood. In verse 14, however, it is a full word (the adjective 'better') that is missing in the second line, seeming to give a metre 3+2, but in fact the missing adjective can still be counted, supplying as it were a silent beat. In verse 15 the sentiment of the second line is similar to that of the first, but the words used do not balance those in the first line, as in most of the other verses they do. In verse 16 the words do balance each other, but their order in the second half is reversed (a case of chiasmus, not always reproduced in English, though fortunately it is here). Also in this verse the construct state 'length of days' (i.e. 'long life', RSV) is given two stresses, being paralleled in the second line by two separate nouns, 'riches and honour'.

Finally, in verse 17 the construct state 'ways of pleasantness' is again given two stresses, and the word 'all' (which is not always stressed) is in the second line given a stress to make up the number of stressed syllables. It is by such variations that the Hebrew poet rings the changes in the parallelism he is compelled to employ, and shows his skill as a craftsman.

Next, let us savour the quite different atmosphere of Psalm 19.7–10, which is mostly in the longer and much rarer 5+5 metre:

7. The law of the Lord is perfect, reviving the soul;
    the testimony of the Lord is sure, making wise the
        simple;
8. the precepts of the Lord are right, rejoicing the heart;
    the commandment of the Lord is pure, enlightening the
        eyes;
9. the fear of the Lord is clean, enduring for ever;
    the ordinances of the Lord are true, and righteous
        altogether.
10. More to be desired are they than gold, even much fine
        gold;
    sweeter also than honey and drippings of the
        honeycomb.

Verses 7 and 8 are quite remarkably regular, perhaps an attempt to reflect the symmetry and perfection of the law. But the next two verses are much looser, the last three lines especially not fitting into the pattern of a long phrase followed by a shorter; and verse 10 is actually 4+4, winding up the stanza. (Incidentally, the stanza does not formally exist in Hebrew poetry; if we use the term at all, it corresponds to the sense and not to the structure as, for instance, in a Shakespearean sonnet; and it can have any number of lines, unlike a poem of Robert Burns, where the stanzas are all of the same length. Also incidentally, in English we often call such a division a verse, but that term is excluded by the use of 'verses' in the Bible as a reference device for a small stretch of text.)

The short 2+2 metre is not very common, but consider how suitably it is employed (predominantly) in Jeremiah 6.23–6 where the prophet is announcing the approach of an enemy:

> 23. ... They lay hold on bow and spear,
>   they are cruel and have no mercy,
>   the sound of them is like the roaring sea;
>   they ride upon horses,
>   set in array as a man for battle,
>   against you, O daughter of Zion!
> 24. We have heard the report of it,
>   our hands fall helpless;
>   anguish has taken hold of us,
>   pain as of a woman in travail.
> 25. Go not forth into the field,
>   nor walk on the road;
>   for the enemy has a sword,
>   terror is on every side.
> 26. O daughter of my people, gird on sackcloth,
>   and roll in ashes;
>   make mourning as for an only son,
>   most bitter lamentation;
>   for suddenly the destroyer
>   will come upon us.

It is noteworthy that in this poem the parallelism is sometimes not very exact, for example, in verse 25 where 'terror is on every side' answers to 'the enemy has a sword'; and sometimes it breaks down altogether, as in verse 26, the last four lines of which are a long simple statement, merely divided up for the sake of the metre. Also noteworthy is the appearance of triplets in verse 23; in the first set of three lines there is only the loosest parallelism, and in the second set the last line is not parallel to but continues the other two. Clearly the poets of Israel allowed themselves quite a bit of leeway in varying their use both of metre and of parallelism.

An interesting feature of parallelism, in which the Hebrew poet has to repeat himself, is that he has to have at his disposal lists of suitable pairs of nouns or verbs or adjectives or even adverbs to balance each other. Let us look, for instance, at the praising words in Psalm 96:

> *verbs*: sing, bless, tell of, declare, ascribe, worship, tremble, be glad, rejoice, exult;
> *nouns*: song, salvation, glory, marvellous works, honour, majesty, strength, beauty.

Or the complaining words in Psalm 44:

> *verbs*: cast off, abased, made us like sheep for slaughter, scattered, sold;
> *nouns*: taunt, derision, scorn, byword, laughing stock, disgrace.

Or the pleading, contrite words in Psalm 51:

> *verbs*: have mercy, blot out, wash, cleanse, purge, cast not away, restore, uphold;
> *nouns*: transgressions, iniquity, sin, that which is evil, sentence, judgment.

It is almost as though the poet had card indexes for various types of poem. From the frequency with which the same pairings of words occur throughout poems of the same sort, it is apparent that many of them are conventional, part as it were of every poet's stock in trade.

Thus we can in their writings hear differences as between an Isaiah and a Jeremiah, and in a book like Job we know we are in touch with a particularly daring individual poet. But if we look at Isaiah or Jeremiah or even Job more closely, we may have to conclude that it is what they are saying rather than how they are saying it that is distinctive. And in the Books of Psalms or Proverbs we cannot even go as far as this. We can detect the type of psalm or wise saying, but we cannot distinguish between a psalm or proverb by one poet and a psalm or proverb by another. In the case of these books we should not be constantly searching for authors, and if in the case of the prophets we do, it is not by and large because of their poetry, but because of their message or their occasional allusions to particular times. We must remember this all the time when studying Old Testament poetry. It was essentially a social not an individual art, like that of the old tribal story-tellers who were the first initiators of the tales we looked at in the last chapter. Originality is not altogether lacking, but in such a public literature it was not originality that Israelite audiences listened for so much as faithfulness to the old well-loved conventions. In that sense Hebrew poetry, even when as in the case of some of the prophets or a book like Job's we know that there was a significant individual poet involved, is more like folk poetry, the poetry of Scotland's border ballads, for instance, or of the troubadors of mediaeval Spain, than it is like the poetry we study in anthologies of English-speaking poets. As people's poetry, the poetry of the Old Testament is often superb and could hardly be surpassed. But on the language level the accolade belongs, not to individual poets, only a few of whom can be identified, but to the tradition of which they were the guardians.

The rhetoric of judgement

Amos is the earliest of the so-called 'writing' prophets, those of whose preaching a record survives in the Old Testament. We can include with them earlier prophets like Elijah and Elisha, about whom we have stories in the Books of Samuel and Kings, and we can contrast them with the anonymous groups of 'sons of the prophets' gathered together in guilds, of whom we hear from time to time (e.g. 1 Sam. 10.5). These guilds were made up of professionals, often itinerant – the various festivals were a favourite haunt – who gave advice and prognostications for a consideration. Like the pagan prophets of Baal in 1 Kings 18 they often indulged in abandoned or ecstatic behaviour and, when consulted, for instance by the king, about important events, they almost automatically promised success or victory in arms.

Not so the 'writing' prophets and their predecessors like Elijah, who saw it as their task in Yahweh's name to condemn both people and court for their lack of foresight, and to mark out the coming reckoning. Not that they were essentially different in status or behaviour from the guilds. Elijah is mentioned as belonging to a guild (this is the implication of 2 Kings 2.1–12), and most of the 'writing' prophets had their circles of disciples, who were probably the ones who collected and preserved their public preaching; and they too could have visionary experiences. Ezekiel in particular indulges in very odd activities (Ezek. 1.1ff.; 4.1ff.). Even Amos, who claimed that he was 'neither a prophet nor a prophet's son', but a simple herdsman and dresser of sycamores, was probably exaggerating not a little; for he was called a 'prophet' by Amaziah, the king's officer, in chapter 7 and told to go back to Judah (he came from the southern kingdom) and 'prophesy' there instead of meddling in the affairs of the northern kingdom. What Amos probably meant was that he was not a professional prophet in the sense of currying favour with his audience, but spoke Yahweh's word as it came to him. There may be a hint in his claim that he was not, like many of the 'sons of the prophets' or even of a 'writing' prophet like Isaiah, attached to the court or a shrine, but insisted on earning his own living. But in most other respects, notably the poetic manner in which he cast his oracles, he was a prophet like the rest. What above all separated the 'writing' prophets from the others in the couple of centuries or so before the exile was not their practice or way of life but their judgement-laden message; and when the end of the nation's independence came about in accordance with their preaching, it was realized that they had been right, so their preaching survived while the popular and optimistic oracles of the mass of their fellows disappeared from sight.

I do not even think we can say, except by hindsight, that the 'writing' prophets alone 'stood in Yahweh's council', although Jeremiah thought so (Jer. 23.18); all prophets perceived their role in this light, as visiting in their imagination the heavenly council, receiving a message from God, and returning to any who would listen to announce, as his messenger, 'Thus says the

Lord'; and all claimed the assistance of God's spirit (Num. 11.29).

As a literary person, Amos was above all the master of satire, a cruder art form than irony. Irony says one thing and means another; it is often witty and humorous, nor is it necessarily condemnatory, but can serve many purposes as long as it gets people to appreciate the incongruity of what they or others are doing or saying (see further Chapter 1). Satire, on the other hand, though it can make use of irony, is not really a figure of speech: it does not manipulate language but on the whole means what it says; it can be clever but is not generally subtle, being concerned to submit folly and wrongdoing to ridicule and, if possible, to effect a change in those addressed by shame or anger. It was a favourite weapon of the judging prophets, and of none more so than Amos. We do not know on what principle his oracles were arranged, whether by subject matter or date (it was probably, as in other prophetic books, by a mixture of both) but the catalogue effect of his writings is in fact not uncharacteristic of the ways of satirists in other literatures.

Thus in Amos 4.1–3 we have the rich women of Samaria – 'you cows of Bashan' he calls them – unfeeling of the poor outside their gates as from their couches they languidly call to their husbands, 'Bring us another drink'; before long they would be hauled away with fish-hooks and cast out through the breaches in the city wall, which an enemy was about to attack. Then in verses 4 and 5 the picture suddenly changes; the whole people are invited, 'Come to Bethel, and transgress; to Gilgal, and multiply transgression'. These were revered pilgrimage shrines, and he invites them to bring their sacrifices, and shout out the number of their freewill offerings – ' "for so you love to do, O people of Israel", says the Lord God'. There is irony here, but chiefly biting satire; and this time the punishment is not spelled out; it hardly needed to be.

In 5.18 Amos uses a kind of curse formula, 'Woe to you who desire the day of the Lord!', the great day when in the national hope God would come to rescue his people. But he goes on, 'It is darkness, and not light', not at all the kind of thing they had been taught to expect. There is irony in this invective. But there is no irony in the next (rather prosaic) phrase, it is 'as if a man fled from a lion, and a bear met him; or went into the house and

leaned with his hand against the wall, and a serpent bit him.'
There is further satire of this kind in chapter 6, 'Woe to those
who are at ease in Zion' (verse 1), and in a sustained stretch
from verse 4 on:

> Woe to those who lie upon beds of ivory,
>   and stretch themselves upon their couches,
> and eat lambs from the flock,
>   and calves from the midst of the stall;
> who sing idle songs to the sound of the harp,
>   and like David invent for themselves instruments of music;
> who drink wine in bowls,
>   and anoint themselves with the finest oils,
>   but are not grieved over the ruin of Joseph!
> Therefore they shall now be the first of those to go into exile,
>   and the revelry of those who stretch themselves shall pass
>   away.

But perhaps the most vitriolic little cameo of all is in chapter 8
(verses 4–6):

> Hear this, you who trample upon the needy,
>   and bring the poor of the land to an end,
> saying, 'When will the new moon be over,
>   that we may sell grain?
> And the sabbath,
>   that we may offer wheat for sale,
> that we may make the ephah small and the shekel great,
>   and deal deceitfully with false balances,
> that we may buy the poor for silver
>   and the needy for a pair of sandals,
>   and sell the refuse of the wheat?'

A people who acted in this kind of way, yet flocked to the
sanctuary to show their piety, were fiddling while Rome
burned; and judgement could not be far away.

In other prophets we hear from time to time plaintive
evangelical appeals to the people to repent before it is too late
(e.g. Hos. 6.1), and sometimes breaking through their criticisms
and threats come words of comfort and hope (e.g. Isa. 11). But
to Amos, the unbending and harsh herdsman turned prophet,
things in his day had gone too far for there to be any hope of

renewal. There is hardly any evangelical appeal in his preaching (perhaps Amos 5.14–15, but notice the 'may be') and only (in the last chapter, if 9.8 and 9.11ff. were not added by his disciples) the slightest trace of hope; the prospect is bleak, and doom is writ large everywhere around. The hammer blows of his satire are tinged with despair. He is the hard man among the prophets, but how powerful is his invective! Even today we cannot read his book without shuddering.

The rhetoric of comfort

The note of comfort, of a more hopeful future to come, is not prominent among the pre-exilic prophets, and in Amos (as we have seen) it is almost completely missing. It only comes into its own after the blow of exile had fallen, when the homeland was under foreign domination, and Jerusalem was but a shadow of her former self. Both Jeremiah and Ezekiel at the beginning of the exile are still full of judgement, rubbing in their 'I told you so' lesson; but they do turn themselves to speculation about the future much more than their predecessors. Jeremiah looks forward to a return, when God will make a new covenant with his people and give them a new heart (Jer. 31.31–4). And Ezekiel gives a detailed description of the restored temple which will take the place of the one destroyed by Nebuchadnezzar (Ezek. chapters 40ff.). But the prophet of comfort *par excellence* is the pseudonymous Second Isaiah, who lived in exile and whose oracles are preserved in chapters 40–55 of the present Book of Isaiah. He doubtless belonged to an Isaianic school which had been founded by the original Isaiah in King Hezekiah's time nearly two centuries previously.

These sixteen chapters form a sustained visionary drama, not acted on a stage of course, but seen in the prophets' imagination. The little huddle of exiles whom he is addressing are invited to share it scene by scene. There is first in 40.1–11 the message of God's advent, declared in the heavenly court and carried down to Jerusalem, the goal of any return; then variously thereafter there are summoned to the divine presence the coastlands, the foreign nations and their deities, their rulers, Babylon the conquering power, even King Cyrus of Persia, whose policies facilitated the return; and mingled with these, Jacob and Israel (the names used for the exiles), distant

Jerusalem (pictured as a bereft mother welcoming her children home) and a special character called the 'servant of the Lord' (probably an ideal Israel). All of these in turn present such case as they think they have, and hear from God what he is about to do, and what their part in the coming deliverance is, negatively or positively, to be. The scenario of course takes place only in the prophet's mind; none of the *dramatis personae* (except a few dejected exiles) actually appears. As far as they are concerned, the prophet (speaking for God) sometimes remonstrates and argues with them (as in 40.21ff., 'Have you not known? Have you not heard?', but chiefly he directs them to God in council, who speaks for himself, and above all his message is one of comfort.

Comfort is the main subject of the prophet's astounding first oracle in 40.1–11, as God's first words are addressed to the denizens of the heavenly court:

> Comfort, comfort my people, says your God.
> Speak tenderly to Jerusalem,
>   and cry to her
> that her warfare is ended,
>   that her iniquity is pardoned,
> that she has received from the Lord's hand
>   double for all her sins. (Isa. 40.1–2)

The recipient is to be Jerusalem, not the exiles, though they are looking on as Jerusalem is addressed. Her warfare, her time of conflict, has come to an end; for God is about to make his appearance, and lead his exiles home. The word 'double' should not be taken too literally; it is hyperbole, and means no more than that Israel has suffered sufficiently for their past mistakes.

An angelic voice next speaks, and note that it is not crying in the wilderness, but simply crying to his companions:

> In the wilderness prepare the way of the Lord;
>   make straight in the desert a highway for our God. (verse 3)

The New Testament use of this quotation in Matthew 3.3 (and parallels) touches it up to make it refer to John the Baptist. Second Isaiah knows no voice crying in the wilderness; rather it is in the wilderness that a way has to be cleared. The angels have to level the ground and make it even, so that God's progress may be direct and obvious to all.

Another angelic voice (verse 6) then calls for a proclamation, and yet another (not 'I' as in the RSV, but 'he' as in the Hebrew text; the prophet is describing the scene, not himself involved in it) asks, 'What shall I cry?' He is told to announce (to no one in particular, but again the exiles are listening) that all fleshly designs are but grass, and only God's purpose, which is now being fulfilled, shall stand (verses 7–8).

The news finally reaches Jerusalem and the holy city in turn passes it on to her daughter cities (verses 9–10):

> Behold, the Lord God comes with might,
>   and his arm rules for him;
> behold, his reward is with him,
>   and his recompense before him.

At last the exiles are brought in, for this coming God is a mighty warrior bringing his trophies of war with him, and what can these be but his returning exiles? Then in verse 11 the picture changes to one of exquisite tenderness, as God becomes a shepherd and the exiles his flock, which he leads home to the safety of the fold at the close of the day. The tired and weary lambs he carries in his arms and he gently prods the pregnant ewes.

The background to this lyrical outburst, so reminiscent of many of the psalms (the Isaianic school of prophets is as a whole period partial to the Book of Psalms) is the despair of a broken people in exile in Babylon. It is no longer the arrogant and self-indulgent Israel of Amos' day, needing to be woken up to their parlous situation. Comfort and hope are what the people now require, not satire and judgement. Probably their staple religious diet at this time was the lamentation psalms, psalms like 137 composed in exile or just after ('By the waters of Babylon, there we sat down and wept, when we remembered Zion'); and cries of pain must constantly have been on their lips, cries like those of the Book of Lamentations, composed in Judah just after the destruction of Jerusalem, for example 1.12 'Is it nothing to you, all you who pass by? Look and see if there is any sorrow like my sorrow' or, particularly apposite to Second Isaiah, verse 2, 'she has none to comfort her'. Now at last, seventy years after the deportation, they hear a positive rhetoric: Yahweh is stirring and comfort is at hand, he is about to lead his people home in a miraculous new exodus, straight through the desert and this time with no obstacles in the way.

The note of judgement may be more insistent in the prophets as a whole, but the note of comfort is also there, and so appealingly is it sounded that it all but drowns out the other.

The rhetoric of praise

In the Psalms we hear, not the voice of God or a prophet speaking for him, but that of the people of Israel singing to God in the temple. Many of the headings to the psalms give musical instructions about how they should be sung, and not a few have the superscription 'of David', sometimes including an indication of the occasion in his life when he was thought to have composed them. But the headings were added much later and belong to an age at the end of the Old Testament period or, indeed, after it when, following the classical model, books were automatically assigned to authors. It was then that the view became current that David wrote the psalms, just as Moses wrote the Pentateuch and Solomon the Book of Proverbs. We should be very wary of the psalms headings, at least in this regard. It is much more likely that the Book of Psalms was a long time in the making, and that they were composed by the temple staff on this or that occasion over several centuries.

Here we are more interested in who did the singing, whether the people joined in or whether the choir, accompanied by an orchestra (see Ps. 150), were responsible for all the temple music. We do not know for sure; but there are several indications that the psalms were sung antiphonally and that some parts may have been reserved for the congregation. Thus in Psalm 121 someone (the choir perhaps or a priest) begins with a question:

> I lift up my eyes to the hills.
> From whence does my help come? (verse 1)

and someone else (the congregation perhaps) replies:

> My help comes from the Lord,
> who made heaven and earth (verse 2)

The hills, a favourite locale of pagan worship, are apparently here contrasted with God. This is a pilgrimage psalm, and either the choir or the gathered pilgrims forming the congregation, go on (verse 3), 'He will not let your foot be moved ...'; or perhaps it is a priest blessing the pilgrims, 'May he not let your foot be moved...'. There are also hints here and there that some liturgical action is taking place alongside the singing, for example, an entrance procession in Psalm 100, 'Come into his presence with singing!', 'Enter his gates with thanksgiving, and his courts with praise!'. A substantial procession also seems to be being described in Psalm 68.24–5, 27, in which the people, arranged by their tribal names, are involved:

> Thy solemn processions are seen, O God,
>   the processions of my God, my King, into the sanctuary —
> the singers in front, the minstrels last,
>   between them maidens playing timbrels:
>
>   . . .
>
> There is Benjamin, the least of them, in the lead,
>   the princes of Judah in their throng,
>   the princes of Zebulun, the princes of Naphtali.

Presumably the laity processed up to the temple, but did not go into it, for it was kept for the priests, the laity assembling in the courts outside.

Some of the vocabulary of the psalms is also revealing. We have already remarked that the AV's magical phrase 'in the beauty of holiness' (Ps. 96.9) may in fact refer to rich vestments (see Chapter 1). It is probable that the word 'worship' in the same line (and often elsewhere) is more precisely rendered 'prostrate yourselves' (i.e. do the oriental prostration), and the word 'tremble' in the following line in fact may mean dance. It seems that worship in the temple courts was a colourful business, with plenty of activity and involvement by the congregation. The Book of Psalms was, after all, a people's songbook, not a collection of religious lyrics for private appreciation; and they are replete with the conventional language which over the centuries the people had come to treasure as the best means of celebrating their debt to Yahweh, and of bringing their supplications before him. It is the same people that the prophets so mercilessly berated, but we see them at worship in a more attractive light.

The primary note struck by the psalms is praise, reflecting ordinary folk's joyous and almost childlike delight in the presence of their God. There are two kinds of praise in the psalter, narrative praise and descriptive praise. Narrative praise is in effect thanksgiving, as in Psalm 116:

> I love the Lord, because he has heard
> my voice and my supplications. (verse 1)

The psalmist looks back on his past life before turning to God:

> The snares of death encompassed me;
> the pangs of Sheol laid hold on me;
> I suffered distress and anguish.
> Then I called on the name of the Lord:
> 'O Lord, I beseech thee, save my life!' (verses 3–4)

Then, after some lines praising God's mercy, he gives a report of his deliverance (verses 8–11):

> For thou hast delivered my soul from death,
> my eyes from tears,
> my feet from stumbling;
> I walk before the Lord
> in the land of the living.
> I kept my faith, even when I said,
> 'I am greatly afflicted';
> I said in my consternation,
> 'Men are all a vain hope.'

The straightforward interpretation of this psalm is that the psalmist, writing for any individual worshipper who might wish to make it his own, was at death's door; he had found no human help; but God restored him to the 'land of the living'. Because of this he launches (verses 12ff.) into a long paean of thanksgiving, which takes the form of a vow to offer a sacrifice 'in the presence of all his (God's) people' and publicly acknowledge what the Lord had done on his behalf. The psalm is not talking about death and resurrection, but of recovery after a mortal illness.

There are other thanksgiving psalms in which the nation as a whole praise God for their deliverance. These are distinguished from the individual thanksgivings by using the pronouns 'we' and 'us' instead of 'I' and 'me'. An example is Psalm 124 which, before it became a pilgrimage psalm (the heading is 'A Song of Ascents') was clearly composed to celebrate a victory of Israel over some enemy:

> If it had not been the Lord who was on our side,
>   let Israel now say —
> if it had not been the Lord who was on our side,
>   when men rose up against us,
> then they would have swallowed us up alive, ... (verses 1–3)

> (but) Blessed be the Lord,
>   who has not given us
>   as prey to their teeth! (verse 6)

But most psalms of praise are more objective than these two; they do not tell a little story about my or our need of the moment, but are more directed towards celebration of this or that divine quality or attribute almost for its own sake. It was these psalms (about thirty all told) which above all gave the name *Tehillim* ('The praises') to the Hebrew Psalter. The worshippers' thoughts are turned away from their own troubles (so much in evidence in the laments) or even God's deliverance of them from their troubles (as in the thanksgivings) towards contemplation of him who alone in the Old Testament – and not humankind – is the measure of all things.

The structure of the psalms of descriptive praise is very simple. They begin with a call to praise addressed to the worshipper's own self ('Bless the Lord, O my soul') or, indeed, to the whole creation, whom the worshippers represent, or even the company of heaven. There follows in the shorter examples a brief statement of the reason for praising, as in Psalm 100, which is in effect two little calls and two little reasons placed one after the other ('Know that the Lord is God!', 'For the Lord is good'). But in the longer examples the brief statement is expanded, often at some length, to give us a picture or a number of pictures of God's nature or providence. Finally, there are usually some lines of resolution; in Psalm 113 this is merely a repetition of the *Hallelujah* ('praise the Lord') with which the psalm began; in Psalm 103 it is a second call to praise addressed not, like the one at the beginning, to the worshipper's own soul, but to the angels and denizens of heaven; while in Psalm 104 there is a little prayer that God's will be done, that the psalmist's meditation may be accepted and, rather incongruously in such a joyous song, that sinners may be consumed from the earth.

Rather surprisingly, in view of the attention given to Israel's history in the long prose first half of the Old Testament and, whether in warning or in consolation, in the prophetic corpus, the psalms which Israel sang in the temple concentrate, especially in those devoted to the praise of God, on God the creator rather than on the God of Israel. Not that his goodness to Israel is neglected; see Psalms 135 and 136 which both, especially 136, rehearse his mighty acts in the deliverance of Israel at the exodus and thereafter his choosing them as a special people and giving them their land as a heritage. But more often it is God as King that is praised, and as King of the gods, who created the world and sustains all humankind, rather than as King of Israel. Thus in Psalm 93.1ff.:

> The Lord reigns; he is robed in majesty;
>   the Lord is robed, he is girded with strength.
> Yea, the world is established; it shall never be moved;

or Psalm 96.4:

> For great is the Lord, and greatly to be praised;
>   he is to be feared above all gods.
> For all the gods of the peoples are idols;
>   but the Lord made the heavens.

There is polemic against other gods here, but Yahweh's superiority over them is due not to the fact that he favoured Israel, but to the fact that he created the universe.

Sometimes God's role in Israel's life is combined with his role in the world's, as in Psalm 147. But more often his creation of the world and his providence over everyone, and not just Israel, and over the animals and the physical world, and not just humankind, are the proofs of his greatness. Thus in Psalm 104 (almost a poetic version of Gen. 1) he covers himself with light as with a garment, and stretches out the heavens as a tent, rebukes the waters and sets a bound for them, causes the grass to grow for the cattle as well as plants for man to cultivate, even sets Leviathan, the fearful monster of chaos, in the sea to be his sport:

> O Lord, how manifold are thy works!
>   In wisdom hast thou made them all;
>   the earth is full of thy creatures.
>
> These all look to thee,
>   to give them their food in due season. (verses 24, 27)

Another remarkable feature of the psalms of praise is their bias towards the poor and neglected. God's characteristic *modus operandi* is described in Psalm 113: God's name is to be praised 'from the rising of the sun to its setting' (verse 3) because

> Who is like the Lord our God,
>   who is seated on high,
> who looks far down
>   upon the heavens and the earth?
> He raises the poor from the dust,
>   and lifts the needy from the ash heap,
> to make them sit with princes,
>   with the princes of his people.
> He gives the barren woman a home,
>   making her the joyous mother of children. (verses 5–9)

His majesty is geared towards a definite end. He looks down from above the heavens and sees the enormity of human need, the examples chosen being the poor around the rubbish dumps outside Palestinian villages and the woman enduring the ancient curse of barrenness; and their fortunes are changed. It is an overriding concern of God to reverse human values, and in the psalms he is praised for it. Compare Hannah's song after the birth of Samuel in 1 Samuel 2, probably chosen by her from the hymnbook of the shrine at Shiloh, and Mary's Magnificat from one of the New Testament's most Hebraic chapters (Luke 1). In a patriarchal society it cannot be by chance that women are singled out for God's special favour in Psalm 113. And the same is true of the poor; the word here can hardly be spiritualized, as in Matthew's version of the Sermon on the Mount,

'Blessed are the poor in spirit' (Matt. 5.3) compared with Luke's 'Blessed are you poor' (Luke 6.20). It is the world's real poor who are meant.

The rhetoric of lament

The voice of lament is archetypal in the Old Testament. In Christian circles it tends to be ignored or spiritualized or even suppressed, and to their severe impoverishment; for it encapsulates the pain of faithful souls under God's stern providence, and sets before him their insistent 'Why?' – 'Why is the world getting no better', 'Why is there so much undeserved suffering and anguish in human lives', 'Why is God doing nothing about it?' But in the Old Testament it is there from the beginning. Its characteristic vocabulary is present as early as the exodus story, when the children of Israel cry out in their affliction and groan because of their taskmasters (Exod. 3.7); it is there in the prophet Jeremiah (8.22, 'Is there no balm in Gilead?') in the little book of Lamentations (3.19, 'Remember my affliction and my bitterness, the wormwood and the gall!'); in the Book of Job (3.20, 'Why is light given to him that is in misery'); and preeminently it is there in the psalms of lament.

The structure of these psalms is again straightforward. There are, as with the thanksgivings, two sorts, individual (with 'I') and communal (with 'we'). There is no declaration of praise or thanksgiving at the beginning, though there may be at the close. But the following three elements are usually included: first, the lament or complaint itself, with its three participants – the worshipper in his differing needs and the two others, God and the human enemies whom he accuses of being responsible for his troubled state; second, a declaration of confidence that the God who had put him in that state was nevertheless able to heal or deliver him (there are several small psalms based on this confidence section, notably Psalm 23, 'The Lord is my shepherd'); and third, an appeal or request to God to change his mind and be merciful, to release the worshipper from his misery and to deal with, even punish, those human foes who were misusing him. The psalms of lament, belonging to a context of worship, are, not surprisingly, not wholly pessimistic; they have been well called 'strategies for consolation', means by which the worshipper can inveigle God into helping him; but they begin and are often largely taken up with his distress and despair.

The tone varies from the plaintive to the bitter, from the reproachful to the angry. Probably their most enduring feature is the variety of pictures they bring before us of the human condition at most times and in most places – sickness, alienation, loneliness, persecution in the case of an individual, defeat, disaster, exile in the case of the nation.

Let us look a little more closely at Psalm 44. The confidence section most unusually begins this communal lament. Taken on their own the first eight verses celebrate in fine, if rather triumphalist, words the giving of the land to God's chosen people and the continued military success which Israel had enjoyed down the generations – and in both cases the glory is unambiguously given to God, so that they could now boast in him and sing to him for ever. Or could they? It is at once clear when the long lament section begins at verse 9 that such confidence lay in the past. There is irony abroad. The confidence section is not so much a hope for the future as a recognition that such trust had recently been misplaced.

Psalm 44 is a lament following a shattering defeat in battle; the circumstances are now unknown, but we are certainly made to know how Israel felt. This time their God had *not* gone out with their armies, but had delivered them into the hands of their enemies, selling them (verse 12) for no high price. It is a blasphemous suggestion. But there is worse to come; they should have understood this if they had been false to the covenant, but they had not – and God (verse 21) knew this very well. There follows the verse quoted quite out of context by Paul in Romans 8.36 (AV):

> Nay, for thy sake we are slain all the day long,
> and accounted as sheep for the slaughter.

The Christian apostle makes the persecution of believers a cause almost of rejoicing, because in all things they were more than conquerors through him that loved them. But this psalm, with appalling insolence, suggests that it was God's fault that so many of Israel's fighting men were slain; 'for thy sake' should be translated 'because of you'.

The last four verses comprise a final angry and bitter appeal to God to wake up from his sleep, 'Rouse thyself! Why sleepest thou, O Lord? Awake! Do not cast us off for ever!', to see the humiliation of his people and come quickly to their aid. This image of God awaking is usually a comforting thought – indeed 'he will neither slumber nor sleep' (Ps. 121.4) – but here the implication is that God was neglecting his covenantal duty to look after his own (see further Chapter 6, p. 127).

Psalm 44, with its words of scathing anger and of faith on the verge of collapse, marks along with Psalm 88, an individual lament of equal impertinence and equal despondency (it has no confidence section), the nadir or lowest point of certitude in the Psalter. But marvellously faith is not abandoned; both were sung in the temple, and God does not cease to be worshipped.

There are things hard to take in the psalms of lament. The most distasteful is their hatred of the 'enemies', whether the individual's or the nation's. Thus in Psalm 109 this curse is pronounced by the worshipper on his accuser:

> May his days be few;
>   may another seize his goods!
> May his children be fatherless,
>   and his wife a widow!
>
>   . . .
>
> May his posterity be cut off;
>   may his name be blotted out in the second generation!
>
>   . . .
>
> and may his memory be cut off from the earth! (verses 8–9,
>   13, 15)

Even more blood-curdling, especially as it follows hard on the poignant cry of the exiles beneath the willows ('If I forget you, O Jerusalem, let my right hand wither!') is the fate wished on Babylon in Psalm 137.8–9:

> Happy shall he be who requites you
>   with what you have done to us!
> Happy shall he be who takes your little ones,
>   and dashes them against the rock!

These vengeful sentiments, so emotionally expressed, cannot be accepted today, and it were better if they had not been said.

Also hard to take – and certainly going against the grain of Christian piety – is the fact that the suppliants and protestors in the psalms of lament do not confess their sins very often. A small group of seven psalms became known in Christian liturgical practice as the Penitential Psalms (they are 6, 32, 38, 51, 69, 102 and 130), but it seems that they were chosen, not as representing a major psalm theme, but because the Church had some difficulty in finding enough psalms with specific acknowledgement of sins for its purposes. Indeed, if we examine the seven more closely, only Psalms 32 and 51 have the confession of sins as their chief subject; in the others it is but one of the troubles assailing the suppliant. On the other hand, we find that protestations of innocence are not rare, for example Psalms 17.1–3, 5 ('thou wilt find no wickedness in me'), Psalm 26.1, 4–6 ('I wash my hands in innocence') and, already mentioned, Psalm 44.17–18 ('All this has come upon us, though we have not forgotten thee, or been false to thy covenant'). This mixture is perturbing; but it has its positive side. I am not suggesting that claims to rectitude should find a place in our worship, but perhaps, if we are honest, confession of sins and the desire for forgiveness is given too much space; why should God's faithful people have to go on so much about their unworthiness? It is not realistic, it can sometimes be unhealthy, and it is not the Old Testament's way.

The same is true of disapproval of criticism of God. Too much can be made of it. Christians are careful in worship to keep any note of impatience or resentment out of their voices. It is not that we feel none, for when tragedy strikes our own personal lives, we are as apt as the next one to cry, 'Why me?', 'How could God do this?' But we do this in private, and do not allow our frustrations to surface in worship. Every psychologist will remind us that to suppress strong emotion can be dangerous. Perhaps we need more than we think we do the robust openness of the psalms of lament. They sometimes cross the threshold of blasphemy, so keenly are the emotions of abandonment and anger felt. But in the last resort these psalms are presenting humanity's case against God – and the parlous state of the world today shows that he has a case to answer. Christian rhetoric does not articulate that case enough.

A final reason why lament should not be neglected is theological; it stretches our ideas of salvation. In the psalms of lament it is the cry of humanity that triggers the divine response. The charter event of the exodus underlines this. The Hebrews cry out in the misery of their bondage, and God hears their cry and comes down to rescue them. There is no mention of judgement except upon the Egyptians, no mention of the people's sin or of their deserving what they had been suffering. That comes later when the people prove ungrateful, and cast covetous eyes behind them to the flesh pots of Egypt. The initial pattern of salvation in the Book of Exodus – and in the lamentation psalms – is not conviction of sin followed by confession of guilt followed by the word of forgiveness, but experience of affliction followed by cry for help followed by divine intervention. Of course, the first pattern is there in the Old Testament, even in the psalms of lament, compare Psalm 51; but this second one needs a hearing too. God is every bit as interested in removing humanity's poverty and slavery as he is in removing their sin and guilt, and his compassion in itself is enough to move him to action. Remonstrating with him can be a way, if a particularly rugged way, of arousing that compassion. Christians should admit that they may be wrong in setting aside the psalms of lament and in not recognizing the authentic pattern of salvation enshrined in them.

The rhetoric of confident wisdom

The wise men or sages of Israel, as in other ancient societies, fulfilled an important role. They created and preserved its ideal of the good life, concerning themselves chiefly with what comprised acceptable and unacceptable conduct, and summarizing their teaching in pithy sayings, which could easily be remembered. They were not priests or prophets or psalmists, being content to leave the religious side of the nation's life largely to them. It is not that they were irreligious. They believed that the fear of the Lord was the beginning of wisdom (Prov. 1.7; 9.10) but, having accepted that, they concentrated on the human behaviour which such a belief entailed. Wisdom might be God's gift, but it had to be learned and cultivated, and that was where their task came in. In their eyes the opposite of the wise man was not so much the sinner or the wicked but the fool. As time went on their contribution was more and more brought within the concerns of the religious establishment; the torah or law, also concerned with morals and manners but presented as God's word, became more prominent in their teaching, and the two classes of individual could be called the righteous and the wicked as well as the wise and the foolish; but the wisdom movement never fully lost its secular tendency, its interest in man as man, a member of the human race, rather than as man as Israelite, the recipient of favour and instruction from above.

In the Book of Proverbs we see the movement at its most conventional and confident. The great patron of the sages was Solomon who, according to tradition, was the wise man *par excellence*, though his reputation in that area is historically not exactly deserved. It is most unlikely that he composed the Book of Proverbs. If there is any truth in his reputation, it is that he encouraged the wise men, even introducing them into his administration as counsellors, and founded the patrician schools where they taught and where young men were trained to become leading citizens and civil servants. The Book of Proverbs, though in its finished shape much later than Solomon, may well have been built on what went on there, for it is set forth as an educational programme for young men ('my son' the teacher calls them). Most of it from chapter 10 onwards consists of a collection of wise sayings by many unknown sages over the years which probably formed the basis of wider lessons and discussion. In chapters 1–9, which is made up of longer discourses about wisdom and its usefulness, we may have examples of such extended teaching.

Thus the young student is told by a personified wisdom in chapter 8:

> I, wisdom, dwell in prudence,
>> and I find knowledge and discretion.

> . . .

> By me kings reign,
>> and rulers decree what is just;

> . . .

> I love those who love me,
>> and those who seek me diligently find me.

> Riches and honour are with me,
> > enduring wealth and prosperity.
>
> > . . .
>
> I walk in the way of righteousness,
> > in the paths of justice,
> endowing with wealth those who love me,
> > and filling their treasuries. (verses 12, 15, 17–18, 20–1)

Folly, on the other hand, is portrayed as a prostitute lying in wait for the simple, for the young man who is devoid of understanding. This is what is said of her and her victim in 7.21–3, 26–7:

> With much seductive speech she persuades him;
> > with her smooth talk she compels him.
> All at once she follows him,
> > as an ox goes to the slaughter,
> as a stag is caught fast
> > till an arrow pierces its entrails;
>
> > . . .
>
> for many a victim has she laid low;
> > yea, all her slain are a mighty host.
> Her house is the way to Sheol,
> > going down to the chambers of death.

Pious references to God are ultimately in the same vein, as in 3.5–6:

> > Trust in the Lord with all your heart,
> > > and do not rely on your own insight.
> > In all your ways acknowledge him,
> > > and he will make straight your paths.

Detached from their context these verses might seem to cast aspersions on human efforts, but in the context of the Book of Proverbs trusting in God and relying on wisdom are the same thing.

The connection is spelled out in 3.19, 'The Lord by wisdom founded the earth', and more fully in 8.27, 29–31 (wisdom speaking):

When he (God) established the heavens, I was there...
when he marked out the foundations of the earth,
   then was I beside him, like a master workman;
and I was daily his delight,
   rejoicing before him always,
rejoicing in his inhabited world
   and delighting in the sons of men.

God had, as it were, built wisdom into the fabric of things, her ways were his ways, and following wisdom was following God's will. Those who looked to wisdom (or to God) as their guide were by the constitution of things bound to prosper, and those who took folly were equally bound to come unstuck.

In Proverbs chapters 10ff. there are dozens of examples of the single sayings that were used to illustrate this philosophy. Formally, alliteration and assonance are widespread as befits sayings circulating by word of mouth. Thus the Hebrew of 15.27 reads

'oker beto botse' (' is a consonant) *betsa'*

which can hardly be reproduced in English ('griever of his house (is) a greedy grasper'). The RSV gives up on the play and changes the word order, employing circumlocution, 'He who is greedy for unjust gain makes trouble for his household.'

The parallelism employed in the sayings can be better appreciated in English. It is usually antithetic, contrasting two types of actor or action:

A wise son makes a glad father,
   but a foolish son is a sorrow to his mother. (10.1)

but synonymous parallelism is also frequent:

He who digs a pit will fall into it,
   and a stone will come back upon him who starts it rolling.
   (26.27)

and synthetic parallelism (continuing the sense, usually making it more precise) is not uncommon:

He who finds a wife finds a good thing,
   and obtains favour from the Lord. (18.22)

Other devices are used, in which exact parallelism can appear, but by no means always, for instance sayings with 'like' or 'better than' or, though it is used more in chapters 1–9, with an imperative:

> Like snow in winter or rain in harvest,
>> so honour is not fitting for a fool. (26.1)

> Better is a poor man who walks in his integrity
>> than a man who is perverse in speech, and is a fool. (19.1)

> Strike a scoffer, and the simple will learn prudence;
>> reprove a man of understanding, and he will gain
>>> knowledge. (19.25)

> Train up a child in the way he should go,
>> and when he is old he will not depart from it. (22.6)

In chapter 30 there are a number of longer, especially numerical, sayings, which are not in parallelism and not particularly moralistic, but commenting rather on life's peculiarities, though in their own way they reflect the sage's keen observation:

> Three things are too wonderful for me;
>> four I do not understand:
> the way of an eagle in the sky,
>> the way of a serpent on the rock,
> the way of a ship on the high seas,
>> and the way of a man with a maiden. (verses 18–19)

and in chapter 31.10ff. there is the famous poem on the good housewife ('A good wife who can find?'), which goes on for about twenty verses. These two chapters form a kind of addendum, gathering together some material for which a place could not be found elsewhere.

The skill with which the sayings and longer pieces are framed is considerable; and one cannot but be charmed by their attractiveness and wit or by their sharp delineation of various kinds of people to be emulated: the wise son, who honours his parents and accepts their discipline, the virtuous wife, the faithful friend and neighbour, the man who guards his tongue, the sensible courtier who knows his place – or to be avoided: the scoffer, the proud, the drunkard, the seductress, the quarrelsome wife, the greedy, the tale-bearer. But on the whole it is a utilitarian ethic that is commended and the lesson of enlightened self-interest that is taught. There is a confident air about the sages' pronouncements, an optimism that all is for the best in the best of possible worlds. One gets the feeling that the wise men of Israel have life pretty well taped. If you play the game, you will prosper, whether you give the credit to wisdom or to God – and the opposite is also true. This is particularly seen in the case of the rich and the poor. The rich should acquire their wealth honestly and spend it generously and should remember that it will not last for ever (Prov. 27.24), while the poor should be duly humble and show contentment with their lot. So far so good; but there is a nastier assumption written in, a constant refrain that the rich are wise and good because we can see them being rewarded for their efforts, while the poor through their folly are mostly getting what they deserve. The analysis of society is very shallow. It is the same with health and sickness; the wise attain long life but the sick are hardly mentioned, and no account is taken of undeserved suffering. The venerable author of Psalm 37 (a psalm strongly influenced by the wisdom movement) sums it all up when he says:

> I have been young, and now am old;
> yet I have not seen the righteous forsaken
> or his children begging bread. (verse 25)

The poet Edmund Blunden savagely parodies this verse:

> I have been young, and now am not too old;
> And I have seen the righteous forsaken,
> His health, his honour and his quality taken.
> This is not what we formerly were told.
> ('Report on Experience')

What in fact happens when the neat system of the wisdom thinkers who gave us the Book of Proverbs breaks down? Blunden knew. The writer of Psalm 37 is at least aware that there is a problem, for its first verse reads, 'Fret not yourself because of the wicked, be not envious of wrongdoers!' He is worried that the wicked so often seem in life to get the rewards that ought to go to the righteous. But the Book of Proverbs is too smug by half, and will hardly even acknowledge that there is a problem.

The rhetoric of questioning wisdom

It is something of a relief to discover that the sages of Israel did not all acquiesce in the wisdom movement's practically sound but nevertheless quite unrealistic view of the good life, nor did they, like the author of Psalm 37, take refuge in piety – if things go wrong, God will in his own good time see to it that the inequalities of human existence are ironed out. The writer of Ecclesiastes is driven to scepticism, while the author of the Book of Job steals the alien language of the psalms of lament and resorts to protest. Both are writing later than the 'glad confident morning' of the Book of Proverbs, and both are painfully aware that the foundations have crumbled. Today they – or at least Ecclesiastes – might well have become atheists, but that was not a viable choice in antiquity; so both of them in their different ways put God in the dock for creating the kind of world he did. Certainty has gone, and wisdom is no longer easily accessible. But their rhetoric is still basically wisdom rhetoric, at least in the sense that they show scant regard for the law and other home-grown concerns – Job is actually a foreigner, from the land of Uz – but argue from experience and observation. Indeed, sages themselves, they end up by turning the thinking of their predecessors on its head.

Ecclesiastes or, in Hebrew, Koheleth ('the Preacher') is equated in the book's heading with Solomon, but that, even more obviously than in the case of the Book of Proverbs, is tradition speaking. The contents of the book show us a particularly radical sage who, as he looks out on the world around him, on life, as he frequently calls it, 'under the sun' (1.3, 14; 2.11, 17, 18, 19, 20, 22, etc.), sees only futility and emptiness. His favourite word is 'vanity', which with its cognates like 'toil', 'vexation', 'a striving after wind', sounds like a hammer blow throughout the book. He writes mainly in prose, though it is often a poetic kind of prose and sometimes he quotes a number of wise sayings in poetry, which he may have inherited, but this is not certain. Thus the first line of 7.1 could have come from the Book of Proverbs (cf. 22.1), but hardly the second:

A good name is better than precious ointment;
and the day of death, than the day of birth.

The second line indeed chimes with Koheleth's prose sentiments. All human endeavour is vanity; there are good things in
life, eating and drinking and finding enjoyment in honest toil
(2.24), and a poor and wise youth is better than an old and
foolish king (4.13); but at the end 'All go to one place; all are
from the dust, and all turn to dust again' (3.20). One gets the
feeling that for Koheleth death is a release to be welcomed,
though he wonders even about that prospect; 'who can bring
him (a man) to see what will be after him?' (3.22).

Ecclesiastes has escaped a lot of censure because of the
beauty and fascination of his language, though it is remorselessly pessimistic – 'there is nothing new under the sun' (1.9),
there is 'a time to be born, and a time to die; ... a time to weep,
and a time to laugh; ... a time to embrace, and a time to refrain
from embracing' (3.2–5), 'he (God) has put eternity into man's
mind, yet so that he cannot find out what God has done' (3.11),
'behold, the tears of the oppressed, and they had no one to
comfort them!' (4.1), 'Two are better than one' (4.9), 'For as the
crackling of thorns under a pot, so is the laughter of the fools'
(7.6), 'Be not righteous overmuch' (7.16), 'the race is not to the
swift' (9.11), 'Cast your bread upon the waters' (11.1), 'Of
making many books there is no end, and much study is a
weariness of the flesh' (12.12). Above all, there is the lambent
and haunting meditation in 12.1–8, with its marvellous imagery
of the advent of old age:

> Remember also your Creator in the days of your youth,
> before the evil days come ... (when) the grasshopper drags
> itself along and desire fails; because man goes to his eternal
> home ... before the silver cord is snapped, ... or the pitcher
> is broken at the fountain, or the wheel broken at the cistern,
> and the dust returns to the earth as it was, and the spirit
> returns to God who gave it. Vanity of vanities, says the
> Preacher; all is vanity.

Or is Ecclesiastes so highly prized because its scepticism has
not a little truth on its side, and provides a refreshing change
from the bulk of the scriptural writings, which are so

unfailingly getting at us, and urging us to have faith and hope? It is no surprise to learn that it had some difficulty in gaining entrance to the canon, but most of us can be glad that it did.

The Book of Job had no such difficulties, though it was probably not because poetically it is the glory of the Scriptures, but because, in spite of its fierce invective at the expense of established positions, it had a happy ending in Job's repentance and the restoration of his fortunes. The book in fact was generally interpreted optimistically in both Jewish and Christian circles until relatively recent times. Job endures with sterling 'patience' (see Jas. 5.11, AV) his long dark night of the soul, and wins through; eventually God appears to him, and that encounter convinces him that he had complained too loudly:

> Therefore I have uttered what I did not understand,
>> things too wonderful for me, which I did not know.
>
> . . .
>
> I had heard of thee by the hearing of the ear,
>> but now my eye sees thee;
> therefore I despise myself,
>> and repent in dust and ashes. (Job 42.3, 5–6)

After that his healing and the return of his original wealth and the acquiring of a new family could not long be delayed.

Today's interpreters are more inclined to give the most weight to Job's protests, pointing out that his speeches fill far more space than his recantation, and that his recantation in any case is far from a Pauline recantation, being a confession of ignorance rather than of sin. In his speeches Job heart-rendingly bewails his lot at God's hands:

> Does it seem good to thee to oppress,
>> to despise the work of thy hands
>> and favour the designs of the wicked? (10.3)

> God gives me up to the ungodly,
>> and casts me into the hands of the wicked.
> I was at ease, and he broke me asunder;
>> he seized me by the neck and dashed me to pieces;
> he set me up as his target. (16.11–12)

He has put my brethren far from me, ...
All my intimate friends abhor me,
  and those whom I loved have turned against me.
My bones cleave to my skin and to my flesh,
  and I have escaped by the skin of my teeth.
Have pity on me, have pity on me, O you my friends,
  for the hand of God has touched me! (19.13, 19–21)

But this is hardly a personal complaint only. Rather, Job is compelled by his own experience to argue that God treats everyone with the same unfairness, that the divine face that is turned towards humankind is not benign but malign. So to the modern mind Job emerges as the champion of the oppressed, of all who suffer in God's anything but harmonious world, and takes upon himself the role of defender of human dignity before the assize of heaven. This is the Job who says in chapter 3:

Why is light given to him that is in misery,
  and life to the bitter in soul? (verse 20)

or in chapter 9:

It is all one; therefore I say,
  he destroys both the blameless and the wicked.
When disaster brings sudden death,
  he mocks at the calamity of the innocent.
The earth is given into the hand of the wicked;
  he covers the faces of its judges —
  if it is not he, who then is it? (verses 22–4)

or in chapter 14:

Man that is born of woman is of few days,
  and full of trouble.
He comes forth like a flower, and withers;
  he flees like a shadow, and continues not.
And dost thou open thy eyes upon such a one
  and bring him into judgment with thee? (verses 1–3)

or in chapter 24:

Why are not times of judgment kept by the Almighty,
and why do those who know him never see his days?
(verse 1)

But how do the friends of Job react, his opponents in the debate
around which the book is arranged? They are appalled at his
daring, at the wild words he uses, and they are very perturbed
by their implication that God is inconsistent or, worse, cruel in
his governance of the world. Eliphaz (4.3–4) begins by conced-
ing that Job's life had so far been exemplary – 'you have
instructed many, ... you have strengthened the weak hands
... and you have made firm the feeble knees' – but by the time
Zophar has his turn to speak the appeal to Job to change his
ways is muted and the condemnation of him in terms of
wisdom philosophy clear: 'Know then that God exacts of you
less than your guilt deserves' (11.6). And in the second cycle of
speeches (from chapter 15 on) the mailed fist has come out of
the velvet glove, and all three friends go on the offensive; thus
Eliphaz, 'you are doing away with the fear of God ... Your own
mouth condemns you, and not I' (15.4–6); Bildad, 'shall the
earth be forsaken for you? ... Yea, the light of the wicked is
put out' (18.4–5); Zophar, 'Do you not know this from of old ...
that the exulting of the wicked is short ... he will perish for ever
like his own dung' (20.4–5, 7). It is remarkable how these three
men, who had come long distances to counsel a sick and dying
man (2.11–13), remain to anathematize a hell-bound reprobate.
Job, for all that he is hard to argue with, is fully justified in
dismissing their arguments in 12.2:

> No doubt you are the people,
> and wisdom will die with you

and in exposing their hypocrisy in 13.4, 7–8, 12:

> As for you, you whitewash with lies;
> worthless physicians are you all.
>
> ...
>
> Will you speak falsely for God,
> and speak deceitfully for him?
> Will you show partiality towards him,
> will you plead the case for God?

. . .

Your maxims are proverbs of ashes,
your defences are defences of clay.

The rhetoric of the friends is wisdom rhetoric, though of the
wisdom movement in its later stages, when God is more
directly brought in and when its confident division of humankind into two classes, who can both look forward to the
appropriate rewards and punishments, is not proving easy to
maintain, and is increasingly requiring the cudgels to be raised
in its defence, even to the extent of humiliating humankind to
exonerate God. Yet, in fairness to it, the position of the friends
should not be too lightly dismissed; for making the necessary
alterations, it is still the position of the everyday believer today.
He or she may avoid the vicious condemnatory language of the
friends, but otherwise the believer holds that, generally
speaking, a man will reap in this life, good or bad, what he
sows. Sometimes, however, the wicked prosper and the righteous suffer; but we must not criticize God for this state of affairs
because, though we ourselves may not understand what is
going on, God is still in charge and he will see to it that justice
eventually prevails. This is essentially the view of the old folk
tale which frames the Book of Job and in which Job intones his
renowned sentiment, 'the Lord gave, and the Lord has taken
away; blessed be the name of the Lord' (Job 1.21). But that was
before he went on the rampage against God.

But perhaps we are jumping the gun. Perhaps in the last
analysis this view is Job's view too; and it is the rhetoric of
lament that makes the difference. In the psalms of lament the
bewildered sufferer is allowed to rail at God, and he is allowed
to maintain his innocence. 'I am blameless', Job says in 9.21,
'but it is all the same; God destroys both the innocent and the
guilty' (cf. NEB). That goes against the grain of wisdom
teaching, but it would not surprise in a lament psalm. Insulting
God is part of the plaintive's 'strategy for consolation'; but it
must be accompanied by a recovery of faith to make any appeal
to him genuine. This is exactly what happens in Job's case.

In the first cycle of speeches Job is too far gone in despair to
believe that God would listen to him (9.32) or to ask much else
from him than a quick end to life, as in 10.18, 20–1:

Why didst thou bring me forth from the womb?
  Would that I had died before any eye had seen me ...
Are not the days of my life few?
  Let me alone, that I may find a little comfort
before I go whence I shall not return,
  to the land of gloom and deep darkness...

But in the second cycle he says in 13.3:

  But I would speak to the Almighty,
    and I desire to argue my case with God.

and a little later in the same chapter he backs up his appeal
with a declaration of trust, in the rendering of the Authorized
Version (13.15):

  Though he slay me, yet will I trust in him:
    but I will maintain mine own ways before him.

The RSV, retaining his despair a little longer, translates:

  Behold, he will slay me; I have no hope;
    yet I will defend my ways to his face.

The difference between these two renderings is only one little
word in Hebrew, *lu* 'would that' and *lo* 'not', and both variants
are known in the history of the text. So one can choose between
them on the grounds of one's understanding of the thrust of the
book so far. I prefer, with the older interpretation on which the
AV depends, to see in the verse almost the first stirrings of a
returning trust and hope on Job's part; a modern version like
the RSV, not surprisingly, takes a more negative view.

But it hardly matters. By the end of chapter 16 (verses 18–21)
it is impossible to argue that a subtle change in Job is not taking
place. He sees in his mind's eye a witness who will vouch for
him in an assize in heaven, though he himself may by that time
be dead:

  O earth, cover not my blood,
    and let my cry find no resting place.
  Even now, behold, my witness is in heaven
    and he that vouches for me is on high.
  My friends scorn me;

my eye pours out tears to God,
that he would maintain the right of a man with God,
like that of a man with his neighbour.

His spilt blood will cry out from the ground like Abel's (Gen.
4.10), and God will hear. But, more, his heavenly witness will
argue his cause for him, and force God to change his mind. If
we read the passage carefully, we may even conclude that the
witness is God himself, a kindly God taking on a wrathful God
and wresting from him the verdict of 'Not Guilty' which Job
longs for. This is, in my view, how the next – and celebrated –
appeal two short chapters later should be interpreted (19.23ff.).
Job wishes that he might have after his death a memorial
engraved in the solid rock but (rather than the 'for' of the
RSV), not at all sure that this can come about, he has at the same
time a vision of his redeemer standing on earth (not this time in
heaven) to announce for all to hear his vindication, and he shall
see God with his own eyes, and he will be on his side. This is
the passage immortalized by Handel in the *Messiah*, and I shall
be looking at it again later (see Chapter 6, pp. 136–7), but for the
present it is enough to emphasize that the redeemer, on any
sensible reading of an extremely difficult passage, and God
must be one and the same. God, in response to his heartfelt
pleas and his recovery of faith, gives Job what more than
anything else he wants, a declaration that in spite of all that
seems (in wisdom's logic) to the contrary, he is innocent.

The rhetoric that guides Job most of the time is, most
unusually for a book stemming from wisdom circles, that of
worship – his accusations against God, his requests to God, his
protestations of innocence, his faith in God all derive from the
language of the psalms of lament – and it reveals Job as
primarily a distressed plaintive seeking redress from heaven.
The rhetoric of the book as a whole, especially of the friends but
also sometimes of Job, is wisdom rhetoric. It is concerned with
the conduct of an individual, with the question of reward and
punishment, and with the constitution of things in general. Do
things in general, as discussed in the book, accord with the
conclusions of the wisdom movement and justify its advice?
The answer which at least some wisdom thinkers in ancient
Israel give is 'No'. Ecclesiastes' scepticism and Job's protests
both mortally damage the conclusions from within, and Job in

addition prescribes a better advice, by taking on God but nevertheless appealing to him in faith.

The speeches of the Lord from the whirlwind (chs. 38–42) and their special problems I shall consider in a future chapter (Chapter 5, pp. 101–3).

There are a few other poetic genres, deriving probably from everyday life and practice, embedded here and there in the prose books and used, often in a modified form, in the poetic works. Examples are: Exodus 15 (The Song of the Sea); Numbers 22–4 (Balaam's blessings and cursings before war); Judges 5 (The Song of Deborah); 2 Samuel 1.17–27 (David's lament over Saul and Jonathan); Proverbs 31 (encomium, in praise of the good housewife); Isaiah 14.3–21 (dirge over Babylon); Isaiah 52.13–53.12 (inverted encomium, in praise of a suffering servant); Ezekiel 27 (dirge over Tyre). But the six investigated in this chapter are very much commoner, and sound the chief notes of Old Testament poetry as represented by the Prophets, the Psalms and the wisdom literature. Poetry is also the main vehicle of mythical allusions and of imagery, treated in the final three chapters, though these are sometimes found in prose.

- 5 -

THE RHETORIC OF
HEBREW MYTH

To MOST PEOPLE today 'myth' is an unpleasant word, conjuring up memories of the rather fantastic and even grotesque tales which ancient peoples told about their gods, about where they lived and how they got on – or did not – with each other, and about how they brought the world and its plants and animal and human creatures into being and from afar supervised, in anger or kindness, their various existences. These were serious matters, but it is the far from serious way myth treated them that upsets modern readers and listeners. So in modern parlance the word implies something that is imaginatively over the top, something irrational if not downright untrue; and to religious people especially, it seems hardly conceivable that the Bible should contain mythical language or that the stories at the beginning of Genesis should be called myth.

As far as the Old Testament is concerned there is some truth but also a lot of falsehood in the modern assessment of myth. The truth lies in the fact that the Old Testament speaks of a historical revelation. Israel did not become acquainted with God in speculation of the kind that myth embodies, but in concrete events like the exodus and the exile, and this experience was the controlling factor in the conclusions it drew about his nature and purpose. The falsehood is that Israel was also part of the ancient world; it did not exist in a vacuum but inherited ancient ways of thinking and speaking, and these included the mythological way of looking at things. Thus in its view of the world's geography and constitution it simply accepts the view of its neighbours. There is what we might call primitive science in this, in so far as it is based at least partly on observation, on what looks like a flat earth with the heavens or the firmament superimposed like a canopy over it and joining it at the horizon. But the heavens were also the home of the gods, and this is mythological talk. In Israel's case they naturally become the home of its one God. But he does not only dwell there, but his home is pictured as a city which contains his 'house' or palace or temple, and he is surrounded by his angels, by the 'host of heaven', and by the seraphim and cherubim; and over this realm he rules as king. From heaven he 'comes down' from time to time to earth, which he also rules from his earthly 'house' assisted by his earthly people, Israel, and its earthly king. This whole scenario, with heaven as a mirror-image of earth, is endemic to Old Testament religious rhetoric and is essentially mythological; that we have taken such rhetoric over from the Old Testament and use it to enhance our approach to God in worship does not make it any less so.

But the people of the Old Testament did not only breathe the general mythological atmosphere of their time; they themselves also became mythmakers; and this is, if anything, more perturbing. In the stories of creation, the Garden and the Flood they have parted company with their history, and are talking about things that happened in remoter times before history as they knew it began; and they were not averse to larding these stories with people and things which were unknown in the historical world to which they belonged, with a talking snake in Eden, for instance, or heavenly beings who married earthly women, or a ship shaped like a box which could make room for two of every kind of animal. It is churlish of believers to deny the label myth to such stories, and to pretend that they are something else. They occur in the same book as Abraham and the other patriarchs, but they are not attached to this historical world like the stories we looked at in Chapter 2, being more like the stories we call fables or fairy-tales. They supply, in effect, a non-historical introduction to what happened in the remembered time of Israel's beginnings and its development ultimately into a monarchical state. They are, of course, Hebrew myths, informed by Israel's unique religion and not by surrounding religions; they find no place, for instance, for goddesses (Hebrew indeed, has no word for 'goddess'). But they are still myths, and should be interpreted as such.

The myths of Genesis

The priestly account of creation in Genesis chapter 1 is a particularly cool example of myth. It still has God manually 'separating' the waters to make room for the firmament, 'setting' the stars in this firmament, commanding ('let ...') a dry earth to appear and its vegetation to grow, and 'making' the sea and land creatures and human beings; but it avoids the wilder mythology of the creation references in Israel's poetic literature. Thus Psalm 74 positively revels in the clash of conflict which is almost universally read into the accounts of creation in surrounding mythologies, substituting a monster, which it calls Leviathan or Rahab, for the swirling waters of Genesis 1.2. The priestly authors of Genesis did not like the more lurid furniture of myth in composing their careful account of how the world began, though they still spoke mythologically in what they considered a more fitting way. But in their almost modern delicacy of taste they stand nearly alone in the Old Testament.

Their delicacy was certainly not shared by the authors of Genesis chapters 2 and 3. They preface their story with a much cruder version of creation (2.4–9) and then introduce into it God as the owner of a garden, a talking snake, and a guardian cherub. This story obviously stands nearer to its source in the folk tradition of Israel (cf. the poetic verses in 2.23 and 3.14–19), and it has been considerably less tampered with than the sober creation narrative in chapter 1. It still has about it the marks of a fairy-tale.

The folk story I have chosen to compare it with is that of *Cinderella*, now relegated to the nursery but once appreciated by adults as well. This tale originated in the mists of mediaeval Europe and no doubt had a long oral life before being included in the collection of the brothers Grimm.

We can best analyse the plot of *Cinderella* in terms of a problem to be solved and of the various moves, at first unsuccessful but ultimately successful, by which the solution was arrived at. The first move is the girl's attempt to alleviate her situation by trying to please her wicked stepmother and her two daughters, but this only makes them treat her more cruelly still. The second move is the invitation to the ball given by the king's son which Cinderella, though by birth as eligible as her stepsisters, is not allowed to accept. The third move brings in the fairy godmother, with whose magical help, involving a pumpkin and some rats which turn into a coach and coachmen, Cinderella does in fact go to the ball. But this move is accompanied by a condition ('be back by midnight'), which Cinderella does not quite manage to keep, and in her near failure she leaves her slipper behind. The fourth and eventually successful move is the prince's search for the owner of the slipper, which only Cinderella's slender foot fits. The heroine marries her prince charming and achieves the happiness she deserves.

A fifth and final move can perhaps be seen in the generous way in which (in some versions of the story) Cinderella forgives her stepsisters and finds husbands for them too. This restores the family unity which had been burst asunder when Cinderella's natural mother died and her father remarried, and so fully solves the problem with which the story had begun.

The structure of the Garden of Eden story is amazingly similar to that of the story of Cinderella, though it is a good deal more complicated. It is in fact two separate little stories run together, one in which there is a need to be met and one in which there is a problem to be solved. But in each of the two parts a number of moves can be distinguished leading respectively to the meeting of the need and the solving of the problem. There is also a link between the two parts, uniting them into a single whole. This is supplied by the condition which God (acting almost like Cinderella's fairy godmother) lays down. It is the failure of the hero and heroine to keep this condition which in fact becomes the problem to be solved in the second part and leads to their sentencing. But there is a mitigation of the sentence, which is in some ways like the fifth and final move in the Cinderella tale, introducing a note of mercy to lighten its severity. The subject-matter is of course far more significant than in the story of Cinderella, that of paradise and paradise lost, favourite themes in the mythologies of surrounding peoples, but the structure is typical of all traditional folk tales. It can be represented tabularly as follows:

Act I or Paradise

The Need (2.4–7). God creates man as a 'living being'. The implication of this is that man cannot exist on his own.

Move 1 (2.8–15). The man needs somewhere to live and work, so God creates for him the garden with its trees of immortality and knowledge.

The Condition (2.16–17). The man, however, is forbidden to eat from the tree of knowledge.

Move 2 (2.18–20). The man needs a helpmeet, so God creates the animals to be subject to him and serve him.

Move 3 (2.21–2). The animals do not meet this need, so God creates woman.

The Need Met (2.23–5). The man and woman live together in the garden in harmony and innocence.

Act II or Paradise Lost

The Problem (3.1–7). The man and the woman fail to keep the condition for living in paradise. On the prompting of the serpent they eat of the forbidden fruit and gain knowledge. God has to prevent this threat to his divinity, for what if they should now avail themselves of the fruit of immortality as well?

Move 1 (3.8–13). God confronts the participants. They by their excuses and their accusations of each other show that the harmony of paradise is irrevocably disrupted and its innocence irretrievably lost.

Move 2 (3.14–19). God pronounces on each in turn punishments which draw attention to the enmity, suffering, toil and eventually death which are the inevitable results of knowledge.

Mitigation (3.20–1). Nevertheless, the man and the woman will have children, and God will provide for their needs.

Move 3 (3.22–3). God removes them from the garden to the world outside where, now mitigated but still severe, the sentences can take effect.

The Problem Solved (3.24). Man is banished from paradise and no longer has access to immortality.

Can we go further than comparing structures, and use tales like that of *Cinderella* to help us to interpret the myth of the garden of Eden? I believe we can.

We can be sure of one thing, which is that the people for whom the *Cinderella* story was originally composed – and remember they were adults of several centuries ago, not children of today – did not regard it as a piece of historical reporting. They could have had no conceivable interest in whether a girl of that name ever existed. Indeed, the story itself, by creating a 'never never' setting in which things happened that would never have happened in their real world, actively discouraged them from speculation of that kind.

Yet there was meaning in it for them. Perhaps it encouraged them to think that, if they behaved as graciously as little Cinderella did, happiness and fortune would come their way too. At least it gave them a hope to cling on to amid the tedium and hardship of their everyday lives. In their more realistic moments they would realize that the chances of this happening to them were remote; but what was to stop them having dreams? In its rather sentimental and escapist way the story of Cinderella is a genuine enough parable of the human situation in the dismal society which gave rise to it.

An interpretation of the Garden story can be attempted along the same lines. This would begin by placing its fantastic atmosphere on a similar non-historical footing. In other words, the naive picture of God as potter and landowner, the trees whose magical fruit transferred wonderful gifts, the talking snake, the fierce guardian cherubim, the very Garden itself – all these are but the furniture of the story. There never was such a place as the Garden of Eden, nor was there ever a historical person called Adam who was its gardener and conversed with snakes and with God in Hebrew. The Garden is a garden of the mind, a garden of people's dreams, the kind of place they would like this world to be, the kind of place indeed they know it ought to be, was meant by God to be. And Adam is each one of us, he is Everyman. That this world is not as God planned it is due to humanity's rebellion against God, to the sinful Adam in us all. It is as if every day paradise beckons us, but every day we eat the forbidden fruit and are banished from it, back into the real world with all its toil and suffering and quarrelling.

Interpreted like this the story of the Garden also becomes a parable of the human situation, though on a more profound level than any fairy-tale could aspire to. Both it and the story of Cinderella paint for us a symbolic picture of the mocking contrast that exists between humanity's potential (described in story language as the 'then') and their actual state (described as the 'now'). But whereas the fairy-tale runs out in sentimentality and wishful thinking (as fairy-tales tend to do) the biblical myth deals with weightier matters (as myths usually do) and ends by confronting us with the reality of what the religious insight calls sin.

The following myths in Genesis rub in with increasing ferocity the dire straits into which humanity landed itself in these far-away times beyond memory – the first murder, by Cain of Abel (4.1–16), the founding of the first city by the same Cain (4.17), the list of the predeluvian patriarchs who lived to huge ages (ch. 5) (but one of them, Lamech (5.28), cries out in pain for relief from his toilsome lot), the angel marriages (6.1–6) which by mixing earthly creatures with heavenly gave rise to the giants of old and triggered the Flood (chs. 6–9) in which God all but destroyed the human race, the racism of Noah's sons (9.25–7), the spread of new peoples after the Flood (ch. 10) and the appearance of the mighty hunter Nimrod (10.8–9); and the final enormity (11.1–9), the attempt of human beings to join God at the top of the tower of Babel. With the knowledge they had obtained and the great things they had achieved, they were now in a position to take over God's place and rule the world themselves. God had to move to regain the authority they had filched from him, and the way he chose to do this was to bring Abraham out of Ur and lead him to a new land, where he would become the forefather of the chosen people. History as we know it had begun and the story of salvation set in motion (12.1–3).

But in reality Genesis chapters 1–11 do not tell us of what happened at the beginning of time so much as they describe in the colourful language of myth the parlous state of human beings without God, then no doubt but also now. The metaphorical meaning of the myths concerns all of us all the time, excluded from God's presence until we make our peace with him. Their message is a lugubrious one; they are not at all impressed by human knowledge or the achievements of human civilization, and they tell of a world that has gone sadly wrong.

But they are but a prelude to God's action in the sacred history and to God's action now to redress the disaster. Putting up with the fantasy in which as ancient myths they indulge is a small price to pay for the wisdom which, at a deeper level, they contain.

Myth elsewhere in the Old Testament

The way myth operates in its full narrative form was looked at in the last section. In this section we discuss the more scattered mythological allusions and motifs in the rest of the Old Testament, how they are made to accord with its essentially historical religion, and how, taken as a whole, they impart a very distinctive veneer to its rhetoric.

The chaos battle and creation

Creation in the mythologies of the countries bordering on Israel was usually understood in terms of a struggle between their chief deity and the forces of chaos, represented by a fearsome dragon or monster; and cosmos resulted from its defeat. In the Babylonian myth of creation it is called Tiamat and is female in gender; her name survives in Hebrew, both as a feminine and a masculine noun, as *tehom*, meaning 'the deep, the abyss' (cf. Gen. 1.2). Tiamat is slain in battle by Marduk, the head of the Babylonian pantheon, who is then able to create a new world-order. In the closer Canaanite (Ugaritic) area, though the paramount god El is the creator, the chaos battle is fought between Baal, the god of wind and storm, and Prince Yam (meaning 'sea', as in Hebrew), also called Judge Nahar (meaning 'river', again as in Hebrew); the struggle there is therefore not directly concerned with creation, but with the allied theme of providence, the maintenance of the world which El had created.

We saw in the last section that Genesis chapter 1 refused to have a monster in its account of creation but only the waters of the great deep (called, however, *tehom*). But significantly, though there is no battle, chaos has to be ordered and organized before cosmos can emerge; a conflict of some kind is therefore implied. But we also mentioned that the Genesis story is not representative, and that the Old Testament poets

97

had no qualms about bringing in a monster to their creation references. It is variously called Leviathan (meaning 'twisted, coiled'; it occurs as *Litan* in the Ugaritic texts as the name of an attendant of Yam) or Rahab (meaning 'boisterous') or simply 'dragon' or 'serpent'; and Yahweh has to subdue it before he can continue his work of creation or providence. Sometimes it was enough to have Yahweh bringing the 'sea' or 'waters' or the 'deep' under control, but always in a violent manner.

We have allusions to this more robust form of the creation myth in Psalm 74.12–17:

> Yet God my King is from of old,
>   working salvation in the midst of the earth.
> Thou didst divide the sea by thy might;
>   thou didst break the heads of the dragons on the waters.
> Thou didst crush the heads of Leviathan,
>   thou didst give him as food for the creatures of the
>   wilderness.
> Thou didst cleave open springs and brooks;
>   thou didst dry up ever-flowing streams.
> Thine is the day, thine also the night;
>   thou hast established the luminaries and the sun.
> Thou hast fixed all the bounds of the earth;
>   thou hast made summer and winter.

in Psalm 89.9–11:

> Thou dost rule the raging of the sea;
>   when its waves rise, thou stillest them.
> Thou didst crush Rahab like a carcass;
>   thou didst scatter thy enemies with thy mighty arm.
> The heavens are thine, the earth also is thine;
>   the world and all that is in it, thou hast founded them.

in Psalm 104.5–7:

> Thou didst set the earth on its foundations,
>   so that it should never be shaken.
> Thou didst cover it with the deep as with a garment;
>   the waters stood above the mountains.
> At thy rebuke they fled;
>   at the sound of thy thunder they took to flight.

in Job 26.10–13:

> He has described a circle upon the face of the waters
>> at the boundary between light and darkness.
> The pillars of heaven tremble,
>> and are astounded at his rebuke.
> By his power he stilled the sea;
>> by his understanding he smote Rahab.
> By his wind the heavens were made fair;
>> his hand pierced the fleeing serpent.

The precise details of some of the allusions in such passages are uncertain (e.g. is there a memory of the Canaanite monster Yam in the references to the 'sea'?) but their thrust is clear. They celebrate or appeal to the themes of creation and providence as instances of God's trustworthy power; and in all of them a conflict is described.

The chaos battle as a metaphor of evil

In quite a few passages the chaos conflict is extended to the human sphere, historicized in the events of history or in the lives of individuals, and becomes therefore a symbol of the evil powers which afflicted either the nation of Israel or humanity in general. This kind of comparison is typical of Israel's emphasis on God's revelation in history, which is backed up or illumined by his primordial actions at the time of creation.

We have already mentioned, as an example of hyperbole, Jeremiah 4.23ff. with its picture of chaos-come-again to point up the depredations caused by a foreign invasion. Similarly, in Isaiah 30.7 Egypt is compared to the monster ('therefore I have called her "Rahab who sits still"' as if the fierce dragon of old was becoming lazy); and in Jeremiah 51.34 Babylon ('he (Nebuchadnezzar) has swallowed me like a monster', behaving more like a dragon should). In Psalm 77.16 chaos battle language is used to describe the parting of the sea at the exodus ('When the waters saw thee, O God, ... they were afraid, yea, the deep trembled'); while in Isaiah 51.9–11 the creation battle blends with the exodus tradition as God is urgently called upon to deliver his people in a new exodus from the land of exile:

Awake, awake, put on strength,
O arm of the Lord;
awake, as in days of old,
the generations of long ago.
Was it not thou that didst cut Rahab in pieces,
that didst pierce the dragon?
Was it not thou that didst dry up the sea,
the waters of the great deep;
that didst make the depths of the sea a way
for the redeemed to pass over?
And the ransomed of the Lord shall return,
and come to Zion with singing.

Again, in Psalm 46 an allusion to the violent events of creation illustrates Jerusalem's safety (the inviolability of Zion, the motif is sometimes called):

God is our refuge and strength,
a very present help in trouble.
Therefore we will not fear though the earth should change,
though the mountains shake in the heart of the sea;
though its waters roar and foam,
though the mountains tremble with its tumult. (verses 1–3)

and the nations who dare to attack her take on the lineaments of God's primordial foes:

The nations rage, the kingdoms totter;
he utters his voice, the earth melts. (verse 6).

There is a more general reference in Psalm 93.3–4 to the fierce floods of these mythical days, and it is emphasized that they are no match for Yahweh:

The floods have lifted up, O Lord,
the floods have lifted up their voice,
the floods lift up their roaring.
Mightier than the thunders of many waters,
mightier than the waves of the sea,
the Lord on high is mighty!

Through them all he will protect his own; compare Isaiah 43.2:

When you pass through the waters I will be with you;
    and through the rivers, they shall not overwhelm you.

Perhaps the most problematic reference to the monster(s) is in
the second speech of Yahweh in the Book of Job (chapters 40–1),
with its celebrated descriptions of Behemoth (meaning *the* beast;
it is a hyperbolic use of the plural) and Leviathan. Modern
commentators usually take these beasts to be describing the
hippopotamus and crocodile of Egypt, and therefore understand the second speech of God as continuing the thrust of the
first speech (chapters 38–9). In this God takes Job on a mytho-
poetic tour of nature and asks him where he was when he, God,
laid the earth's foundations, controlled the raging sea (38.8–11;
there are connotations here of the chaos conflict) and created the
morning light; had Job ever entered the gates of death, or visited
the storehouses of the snow and hail, cleft a channel for the rain,
bound the chains of the Pleiades, sent forth the lightnings, or
tilted the waterskins of heaven? Then, turning to the animal
kingdom, God asks Job what he had to do with providing prey
for the lion or bringing into being the mountain goats, the wild
ass, the wild ox (the now extinct aurochs, not the unicorn, which
the translators of the AV thought had a real existence in their
time), the stupid ostrich, the mighty battle-horse, the soaring
hawk and eagle. It is a powerful evocation of the extent of the
heavens as they were believed to be when the book was written,
and of the freer and less biddable creatures of the Palestinian
scene, which God regularly visited but not Job and which God
could control but no human being; and it was clearly meant to
put Job in his place and to remind him of how great was his
ignorance and how small his abilities; and Job admits as much
(see 40.3–5). But it is a reluctant admission, for what had it to say
about his particular problem? So God had to make another
speech.

    To my mind this second speech ought to have dealt with this
problem. Job's real worries were not about God's providence,
but about his justice; and so as it begins the speech seem to do
(40.8–9, 11–12, 14):

    Will you even put me in the wrong?
        Will you condemn me that you may be justified?
    Have you an arm like God,

and can you thunder with a voice like his? ...
Pour forth the overflowings of your anger,
    and look on every one that is proud, and bring him low;
    and tread down the wicked where they stand ...
Then will I also acknowledge to you,
    that your own right hand can give you victory.

The descriptions of Behemoth ('Can one take him with hooks?')
and Leviathan ('Upon earth there is not his like, a creature
without fear') follow after this. But instead of identifying the
two beasts with the proud and wicked, whom only God can
bring to book, most modern commentators go off on a different
tack. In effect they argue that the second speech goes over the
same ground as the first, that Job is humbled not by the strange
if familiar creatures of Palestine but by the even stranger
creatures of more exotic climes. Both speeches refuse to ex-
plicate the workings either of the divine providence or the
divine justice, but leave Job – and us – speechless. They run out
in mystery, and Job's only recourse (42.1–6) is to confess that
God knows best.

I cannot see why Behemoth and Leviathan should not be
interpreted mythologically rather than naturalistically, as in the
examples cited earlier in this section. The modern understanding of God's second speech is too modernistic by half. We know
little about Behemoth, who is not mentioned elsewhere in the
Old Testament. But Leviathan could mean only one thing to
the Israelites listening, a creature of chaos who opposed God
in the beginning and a symbol of the evil which can render
human lives chaotic even now; and presumably Behemoth, like
Rahab, was a similar monster from Israel's primordial lore. The
Egyptian colouring which the poet of Job gives them as
monsters of old would not throw the listeners, who would
straight away realize the point he was making. Behemoth and
Leviathan were *alter egos* of the proud and wicked of earth,
whom God alone could defeat and save a complaining Job from
their clutches. Job in the second divine speech from the whirlwind was being accorded a positive answer to his request. He
was privileged to meet God face to face, and to be told that,
even as he, Job, was impugning his justice, he was combating
the evil in his world and protecting his little ones from
Behemoth and Leviathan wherever they might strike. Job,

while feeling a proper shame at doubting him, could now relax,
knowing that his sufferings had not been caused by God:

> I know that thou canst do all things,
>> and that no purpose of thine can be thwarted ...
> Therefore I have uttered what I did not understand,
>> things too wonderful for me, which I did not know ...
> I had heard of thee by the hearing of the ear,
>> but now my eye sees thee;
> therefore I despise myself,
>> and repent in dust and ashes. (42.2–6)

The violence of nature

Upheaval in nature was not only a symbol of God's enemies
but of God himself, accommodating to himself the duties of
Baal as the Canaanite god responsible for the weather, for the
gentle rain but more often, especially when he was angry, for
downpour, flood and lightning and the trouble they could
cause.

A general picture of Yahweh acting like Baal is given in
Psalm 29.3–5, 8, 9:

> The voice of the Lord is upon the waters;
>> the God of glory thunders,
>> the Lord, upon many waters.
> The voice of the Lord is powerful,
>> the voice of the Lord is full of majesty.
> The voice of the Lord breaks the cedars,
>> the Lord breaks the cedars of Lebanon ...
> The voice of the Lord shakes the wilderness ...
> The voice of the Lord makes the oaks to whirl,
>> and strips the forests bare;
>> and in his temple all cry, 'Glory!'

This is the way his people conceived of him in worship. We
might compare in Psalm 18 the request of a worshipper for
help, which leads into this extravagant description of God
answering his request:

> Then the earth reeled and rocked;
>> the foundations also of the mountains trembled

and quaked, because he was angry.
Smoke went up from his nostrils,
    and devouring fire from his mouth;
    glowing coals flowed forth from him.
He bowed the heavens, and came down;
    thick darkness was under his feet.
He rode on a cherub, and flew;
    he came swiftly upon the wings of the wind ...
The Lord also thundered in the heavens,
    and the Most High uttered his voice,
    hailstones and coals of fire. (verses 7–10, 13)

Baal is also in the Ugaritic texts addressed as 'rider in the clouds' (J. C. L. Gibson, *Canaanite Myths and Legends*, T. & T. Clark 1978, p. 43 etc).

More specifically, in the exodus tradition, thunder and lightning and natural upset are the accompanying signs of God's presence; compare Exodus 19.16, 18:

On the morning of the third day there were thunders and lightnings, and a thick cloud upon the mountain ... And Mount Sinai was wrapped in smoke, because the Lord descended upon it in fire; and the smoke of it went up like the smoke of a kiln, and the whole mountain quaked greatly.

or Judges 5.4–5 (the song of Deborah):

Lord, when thou didst go forth from Seir,
    when thou didst march from the region of Edom,
the earth trembled,
    and the heavens dropped,
    yea, the clouds dropped water.
The mountains quaked before the Lord,
    yon Sinai before the Lord, the God of Israel.

or Psalm 68.7–8:

O God, when thou didst go forth before thy people,
    when thou didst march through the wilderness,
the earth quaked, the heavens poured down rain,
    at the presence of God;

yon Sinai quaked at the presence of God,
the God of Israel.

A further example of this Baal-like trait is provided by the
famous contest between Elijah and the prophets of Baal on Mt
Carmel (1 Kings 18); there is not much violent language, but
Yahweh, in that contest, proves himself a better thunderer
than Baal. It is true that in the next chapter the writers of
Kings go on to make the point, when Elijah experienced an
earthquake:

> but the Lord was not in the wind; ... the Lord was not in the
> earthquake; ... the Lord was not in the fire. (19.11–12)

Rather, he was in the 'still small voice' which followed, presumably the voice of prophecy; or, as some preachers are fond
of suggesting, God is not to be found in the clash of nature, but
in the quiet, internal voice of faith and experience. It may be a
valid point, but it does not cancel out chapter 18 or the myriad
of other allusions in the Old Testament describing upheaval in
nature when God draws near. But that rhetoric does not derive
from observation of nature so much as from a mythological
motif with which the people of Israel were very familiar.
Mountains were expected to quake, thunder to roar, and lightning to flash when God appeared to his people or his presence
was with them.

The council of the gods

We noted in Chapter 2 some of the language used of God in the
Old Testament that brought in other gods, and how it sounds
peculiar to us because it seemed to question the attachment of
Israel to the concept of monotheism. We have also drawn
attention a few times to the council of the gods in heaven, to
the plural form *Elohim*, both 'God' and 'gods', and to the odd
use of the pronoun 'us' in Genesis 1.26 and 3.22. There is
undoubtedly mythology in these usages.

The council of the gods was the place where in other religions
the chief god planned his strategy in consort with the members
of his pantheon. In the Babylonian version of the Flood story
the gods are pictured discussing what they should do about the
human beings whose creation was supposed to supply them

with slaves but who were now annoying them by their for-
wardness and clamour. In the biblical version in Genesis,
however, it is the sin of human beings, not their din, which
leads to the Flood, and in Genesis 6.5ff. God confers with
himself in grand soliloquy and makes up his mind to blot
them out. The priests who composed Genesis 1 or some like
them have obviously been at work here, cutting out the
assembly. Yet despite their susceptibilities, the council
appears as large as life elsewhere, as at the beginning of the
Book of Job where 'the sons of God came to present themselves
before the Lord, and Satan also came among them' (Job 1.6); the
purpose of their meeting was to consider whether the particular
human being called Job was as good as he was rumoured to be.
But probably the most revealing instance for understanding the
way the Hebrews regarded the council is Psalm 82.1, 'God has
taken his place in the divine council; in the midst of the gods he
holds judgment'; the gods are arraigned in this strange psalm
for neglecting their duty to look after the fatherless and the
destitute and, immortal as they were supposed to be, they are
sentenced to death like any human being. They are gods but yet
they are not gods. We encountered a similar fluidity in their
status in the examples discussed in Chapter 2.

The idea of a divine council figures also in Isaiah 40 (see
Chapter 4, p. 63), where the messengers of the assembly are
instructed to take God's decision to rescue his exiled human
people down to Jerusalem; and in Isaiah 6, where the prophet at
his call is transported in his imagination to God's heavenly
temple, and the seraphim perform a cleansing ritual on him to
fit him for his task. Whether or not temple and council are one,
God as though in council then instructs him what to say.
Isaiah's vision is not far from the view all the prophets took
of their sanction for preaching (see Chapter 4, p. 59). In their
minds' eye they visited the divine council and then returned to
earth to announce, 'Thus says the Lord'. See Jeremiah 23.18,
which accuses the false prophets of not having done this.
Compare also 1 Kings 22.13ff. where the prophet Micaiah is
asked by King Ahab to advise him on a forthcoming battle, and
in his reply he has a vision of the heavenly council: 'I saw the
Lord sitting on his throne, and all the host of heaven standing
beside him' (verse 19). God then asks this gathering, 'Who will
entice Ahab, that he may go up and fall at Ramoth-gilead?', and

one of their number, acting like Satan in the first chapter of Job, volunteers. Clearly the answer of this prophet was not going to be to Ahab's liking.

The Lord of hosts

This title is at the start primarily associated with God as commanding the armies of heaven (the word 'hosts' means literally 'armies' in Hebrew), though it can refer sometimes to their human counterpart, the armies of Israel.

In the early traditions of Israel it is the secondary meaning that is foremost. Yahweh, seated on his ark, accompanies the Israelites through the desert, and is present especially in their battles; compare the ancient war-cry preserved in Numbers 10. 35–6 ('Arise, O Lord, and let thy enemies be scattered'). The title is not mentioned in this passage, but it is by David in his taunting of Goliath, the champion of the Philistine forces; 'You come to me with a sword and with a spear and with a javelin; but I come to you in the name of the Lord of hosts, the God of the armies of Israel, whom you have defied' (1 Sam. 17.45).

But even in the early traditions the armies of God's heavenly realms are included in the scope of the title. This is implied in the very physical shape of the ark, which is an empty seat with the back fashioned with carved cherubim (rather fierce beings, quite misunderstood in mediaeval art, where they were painted as chubby little babies). It was clearly an analogue of God's heavenly throne, being occupied by him when he visited his earthly domains, and carried by his earthly army when they went into battle. It was as though, with the cherubim surrounding him, God's heavenly armies hovered above Israel's army to protect them in times of crisis. So in Deborah's song (Judg. 5.20):

> From heaven fought the stars,
> from their courses they fought against Sisera.

So, too, Elisha has to remind his frightened servant, who sees the forces sent by the king of Syria to apprehend his master (2 Kings 6.16–17):

> 'Fear not, for those who are with us are more than those who are with them ... O Lord, I pray thee, open his eyes that he

may see.' So the Lord opened the eyes of the young man, and he saw; and behold, the mountain was full of horses and chariots of fire round about Elisha.

In the prophets, where it is common, the title becomes a more general title pointing up God's holiness and power, for example Isaiah 8.13; Jeremiah 10.16; 32.18. But sometimes its ancient associations with war are recalled, as in Psalm 24.7–10, probably describing a procession of the ark into the temple:

> Lift up your heads, O gates!
> and be lifted up, O ancient doors!
> that the King of glory may come in.
> Who is the King of glory?
> The Lord, strong and mighty,
> the Lord, mighty in battle! . . .
> Who is this King of glory?
> The Lord of hosts,
> he is the King of glory!

Satan and the angel who fell from heaven

In the Garden of Eden story the serpent is not Satan, but one of the beasts of the field 'that the Lord God made' (Gen. 3.1); he represents the animals which in paradise Adam had made and which lived in harmony with him (Gen. 2.19–20), but which in paradise lost were at loggerheads with 'the seed of woman' in a fierce but as yet unresolved struggle in the real world outside. It is not, however, surprising that it was later thought of as Satan; for in the story he is a particularly nasty animal, tempting the woman to wrongdoing. His role is not unlike the role of the Satan (note the definite article in the Hebrew; the word means 'adversary') in the prologue to the Book of Job. The Satan is a member of God's council and his task is to go 'to and fro' on the earth (Job 1.7) seeking cases of human misbehaviour to bring up there and, after sentence has been pronounced, to carry it out. He is not yet God's archetypal enemy, the embodiment of evil; but he is an unpleasant piece of work, by nature suspicious and believing the worst of human beings. On God's instructions he visits all sorts of disaster upon Job. At the end of the book Behemoth and Leviathan take over from him as the personification of the evil which God has to convince Job that he is opposing, perhaps because he is not threatening enough for that job.

The first sign in the Old Testament that he is more than the persecutor in the divine council comes in 1 Chronicles 21.1 where he is now minus the article and incites David to hold a census, something (numbering the holy people) that was God's prerogative alone. So the writers of Chronicles presumably thought, because in the earlier parallel passage in 2 Samuel 24.1 it is God himself who incites David, though in his anger; clearly they did not like this idea. Anyway, *the* Satan of Job 1 acted with God's permission, whereas in Chronicles Satan does evil things on his own initiative.

The final stage in Satan's metamorphosis from a member of God's court, be it a particularly malicious one, into the eternal opponent of God banished from his presence, only comes about after the Old Testament period. But there are hints of how it was arrived at in Isaiah 14.4ff., where Babylon is compared to Lucifer, the morning star, who was cast down from heaven because of his arrogance, and in Ezekiel 28.11ff., where the king of Tyre is likened to an angel who was once in Eden, the garden of God, and because of the 'multitude' of his 'iniquities' was ejected. Incidentally, the Ezekiel allusion suggests that the Garden of Eden in Genesis was an earthly counterpart of God's garden in heaven, and that Adam and Eve were thrown out of it for a comparable lapse to that of the angel ejected from the heavenly one; the author of Genesis 2–3 must have known this myth of a fallen angel and democratized it for his own purposes. But the important thing for us here to notice is that the angel is not Satan either. We can make a guess at what has happened. The creepy serpent of Genesis was identified with the malicious prosecutor of the Book of Job, and both of them were identified with the fallen angel of Isaiah 14 and Ezekiel 28; thus the full Jewish myth of Satan (in Greek *diabolos* or the devil) emerged, to be taken over into Christian rhetoric and, later, into the epic of Milton. But if nothing else, tracing this rather complicated development prevents us from reading the full Christian myth back into the Old Testament. We can take the serpent of Genesis, the Satan of Job, and the angel of Isaiah and Ezekiel at their face values as Hebrew mythological motifs operating independently in their several contexts and interpret them more sensibly in accordance with their roles in these contexts.

Like Behemoth and Leviathan, like Rahab, like the vociferous waters of chaos, Satan in the Old Testament is a type of evil, tempting and preying on humankind, and like them he is at God's disposal, even created by him. But he is not as menacing as they, and not yet fallen from heaven to Sheol, opposing God at every turn, and exulting in his new role as king of the infernal regions, the inveterate foe of all that is good.

Myth, the Davidic king and Jerusalem

Mythological allusions, sometimes obscure, surround the figure of David and his sacred city. The Davidic king's miraculous origin 'from the womb of the morning' is mentioned in Psalm 110.3, and his divine inauguration in Psalm 2.7, 'You are my son, today I have begotten you'. He is God's representative on earth, destined to overcome and rule the whole of it; compare Psalm 72. His city of Jerusalem is impregnable and eternally safe amid the floods of chaos and the attacks of enemy nations (Ps. 46.2–3). Also mentioned in Psalm 46 is a river in Jerusalem, which literally is not true; it is likely that we have here a reference to the river in Genesis 2.10ff. which became four rivers and at whose meeting point was the Garden of Eden. This obscure allusion was probably meant to indicate that Eden was at the centre of the earth, the microcosm, as God's heavenly home and garden were at the centre of the universe, the macrocosm. The transfer of this allusion to Jerusalem is given credence by later references in the Talmud and by the famous map of Madeba, which has Jerusalem at the middle and the other nations grouped around it. Jerusalem's temple too is an analogue of the greater one in heaven. It is built on Zion, God's holy mountain, which replaces Sinai of former times; like the gods of other nations, Israel's God had to have his sacred mountain, by which he 'came down' to earth and whose top was believed to reach heaven. It is a heady mixture of imagery.

But never at any time was Israel a very strong people, nor Jerusalem a place to which the nations flocked to make obeisance, nor their king a ruler far and wide. Indeed, in Israel's own literature they are constantly reminded of their lowly origin, warned against having a king and prepared for the destruction of their holy city and the exile of its inhabitants and the downfall of its king. That was the reality. But in their imagination king and city were invested with a divine aura, and this is reflected in the extravagant language used about them, much of it mythological in nature.

Two hopeful passages in the Book of Isaiah sum up the ideals of the people concerning the city and a new prince of David's line. They refer to the future ('in the latter days') but not the end of the times; it is a future which the people could envisage, a peaceful era which would surely follow the present troubles, when Zion could at last fulfil its God-given purpose ruled over by a *messiah* ('anointed one') sitting on David's ancestral throne:

> It shall come to pass in the latter days
> that the mountain of the house of the Lord
> shall be established as the highest of the mountains,
> and shall be raised above the hills;
> and all the nations shall flow to it, ...
> For out of Zion shall go forth the law,
> and the word of the Lord from Jerusalem ...
> and they shall beat their swords into ploughshares,
> and their spears into pruning hooks;
> nation shall not lift up sword against nation,
> neither shall they learn war any more. (Isa. 2.2–4)

> For to us a child is born,
> to us a son is given;
> and the government will be upon his shoulder,
> and his name will be called
> 'Wonderful Counsellor, Mighty God,
> Everlasting Father, Prince of Peace.'
> Of the increase of his government and of peace
> there will be no end,
> upon the throne of David, and over his kingdom,
> to establish it, and to uphold it
> with justice and with righteousness
> from this time forth and for evermore. (Isa. 9.6–7)

Myth and death

Though, of course, there is no god of death in the Old Testament, there is a surprisingly large number of personifications of the words 'death' or 'Sheol' (the underworld), which have their background in mythology, for example.

Jeremiah 9.21, death as a robber:

> For death has come up into our windows,
>   it has entered our palaces,
> cutting off the children from the streets
>   and the young men from the squares.

Hosea 13.14, death as a gaoler:

> Shall I ransom them from the power of Sheol?
>   Shall I redeem them from Death?
> O Death, where are your plagues?
>   O Sheol, where is your destruction?

(Note the capitals; the AV has 'grave' and 'death' without them. Note, too, the next line, 'Compassion is hid from my eyes'; God is pronouncing sentence of death on his people in this passage and summoning death and Sheol to receive them. It is not a cry of triumph at death's defeat, as Paul makes it in 1 Cor. 15.55.) Compare Psalm 18.4–5:

> The cords of death encompassed me,
>   the torrents of perdition assailed me;
> the cords of Sheol entangled me,
>   the snares of death confronted me.

Job 18.14, death as a king receiving submission:

> He is torn from the tent in which he trusted,
>   and is brought to the king of terrors.

Psalm 49.14, death as a shepherd ingathering his flock:

> Like sheep they are appointed for Sheol;
>   Death shall be their shepherd.

above all, Isaiah 5.14, Sheol as a swallower:

Therefore Sheol has enlarged its appetite
and opened its mouth beyond measure.

Compare Habakkuk 2.5, death as a swallower:

His greed is wide as Sheol,
like death he has never enough.
He gathers for himself all nations,
and collects as his own all peoples.

See also Numbers 16.32, Proverbs 1.12, Job 18.13. It has been suggested that in Psalm 33.19 'the hungry one' should be read instead of 'famine' (the adjective in place of the noun); this small change of vowels would certainly improve the parallelism.

Sheol, the abode of the dead, who, as in other mythologies, are pictured as shadowy wraith-like beings, is a slimy, dark, silent, foreboding place, a pit or a prison, for example:

He drew me up from the desolate pit,
out of the miry bog. (Ps. 40.2)

All of them will speak
and say to you:
'You too have become as weak as we!
You have become like us!'
Your pomp is brought down to Sheol,
the sound of your harps;
maggots are the bed beneath you,
and worms are your covering. (Isa. 14.10–11)

The name of the Canaanite god of death is Mot; except for a full vowel instead of a diphthong, it is the same as the Hebrew word for 'death', *mawet*. In the Ugaritic texts Mot is first of all the deity responsible for natural sterility and summer drought, drying up the ground in the summer season, when Baal's rains failed. There is, as we might expect, nothing of this aspect of his work in the Old Testament; but Mot is also the bringer of human death, and the language used to describe him in that role is not at all dissimilar to that which we have seen used of death in the Old Testament. We might cite the passage in which

Baal sends his messengers to challenge Mot (*Canaanite Myths and Legends*, p. 66):

> Then of a truth do you set your faces
> towards divine Mot
> within his city 'miry'
> where a pit is the throne on which he sits,
> filth the land of his heritage.
> But watch, lackeys of the gods,
> that you come not near to divine Mot,
> lest he make you like a lamb in his mouth.

Mot's reply to Baal's challenge is equally enlightening (*Canaanite Myths and Legends*, p. 68):

> The message of divine Mot,
> the word of the hero beloved of El (is this):
> But my appetite is an appetite of lions in the waste ...
> If it is in very truth my desire to consume clay,
> then in truth by the handfuls I must eat it.

By 'clay' is obviously meant human bodies (cf. Job 4.18–19, 'those who dwell in houses of clay'). See further (*Canaanite Myths and Legends*, p. 76):

> My appetite did lack humans,
> my appetite (did lack) the multitudes of earth.

But there is more to the comparison than words. The challenge issued by Baal to Mot leads to a fight, but significantly there is no open victory. The fierce battle between the two deities issues in a draw, and it takes the intervention of the supreme god, El, to pronounce in favour of Baal. Baal in a way thus wins, but Mot is left in charge of his own territory. El is still king in heaven, and Baal by defeating Yam is his delegated king on earth, but neither is king in the underworld; all they can do is keep Mot at bay and confine his depredations on earth. In particular all human beings when they die become his and remain his thereafter.

This is remarkably like the Old Testament's attitude to death. All human beings at death descend to Sheol and do not return to earth; their spirits may go up to God, but their bodies become

Sheol's and are thought of as passing a shadowy existence under the earth, presumably until they moulder to dust in the grave, and are no more. But what is more disconcerting, Yahweh, like El or Baal, takes no interest in the dead; they have passed beyond his control, as not a few passages in the Old Testament state, for example:

> Turn, O Lord, save my life;
>> deliver me for the sake of thy steadfast love.
> For in death there is no remembrance of thee;
>> in Sheol who can give thee praise? (Ps. 6.4–5)

> Dost thou work wonders for the dead?
>> Do the shades rise up to praise thee?
> Is thy steadfast love declared in the grave,
>> or thy faithfulness in Abaddon?
> Are thy wonders known in the darkness,
>> or thy saving help in the land of forgetfulness?
>>> (Ps. 88.10–12)
> For Sheol cannot thank thee,
>> death cannot praise thee;
> those who go down to the pit cannot hope
>> for thy faithfulness.
> The living, the living, he thanks thee,
>> as I do this day. (Isa 38.18–19)

So, in the last passage, Hezekiah on his recovery; and so we should interpret the several prayers to be saved from death's clutches, in terms, not of resurrection, but of delivery from mortal illness and a return to health and vigour, for example Psalm 116.8–9:

> For thou hast delivered my soul from death,
>> my eyes from tears,
>> my feet from stumbling;
> I walk before the Lord
>> in the land of the living.

The view of death in the Old Testament for the most part is therefore mythological through and through and almost indistinguishable from that of Israel's Canaanite neighbours. It is in its own way a courageous view. Death is the end, a man is gathered to his fathers in whom in a sense he lives on, but there is no immortality for him; his only expectation is for many descendants, and his only hope is while he is here to share in God's eternity. The longing for death as a release by such as Job is unusual; see Job 3.11ff.:

> Why did I not die at birth? . . .
> For then I should have lain down and been quiet;
> I should have slept; then I should have been at rest.

Death in other words was not to be dreaded (at least not too much) but accepted as inevitable; it was its early approach that was feared. A long and happy life was the ideal; that was the prospect held out to Job by his friend, Eliphaz, if only he would change his ways (Job 5.25–6):

> You shall know also that your descendants shall be many,
> and your offspring as the grass of the earth.
> You shall come to your grave in ripe old age,
> as a shock of grain comes up to the threshing floor in its
> season.

Life after death and immortality as something to be yearned for does not come into the picture till very late in the Old Testament. There is a glimpse of it in Job's desire to see God face to face, even if that should not happen till after his death (cf. 19.25ff. in the 'I know that my Redeemer lives' passage); and perhaps in Psalm 139.8 ('If I make my bed in Sheol, thou art there!') and Amos 9.2 ('Though they dig into Sheol, from there shall my hand take them'), though these two passages may simply be figurative descriptions of God's unceasing pursuit of his people in either judgement or mercy (in both passages heaven is also mentioned!). But at least such passages are able to envisage God's presence in Sheol, and that is something new.

However, the first unmistakable reference to resurrection of the dead is in Daniel 12.2 ('And many of those who sleep in the dust of the earth shall awake, some to everlasting life, and some to shame and everlasting contempt'). The logic of faith is beginning to assert itself and to conclude that this life cannot end in nothingness. But the second half of the Book of Daniel is very late; it belongs to the literature called apocalyptic (see the next section). The belief in life after death is, apart from an occasional and forlorn intimation, not an Old Testament belief, but developed among Jews and Christians afterwards; and we should not therefore read it back into the Old Testament period, during which people were bound to the view that death was the conclusion of sentient existence, and that Israel's God may well have willed it so, but he did not extend his power into their underworld abode. His concern was with the living, not the dead.

Myth and the future

The prophetic hope for the future encompassed not only the restoration of Judah after the judgement of exile but rather extravagant claims of a universal victory of God's cause in the conversion of the nations and the inauguration of a reign of righteousness and peace under a messiah of his choosing. These eschatological hopes were anchored in aspects of the pre-exilic religion such as the promise to Abraham that in his seed all the peoples of the earth would be blessed (Gen. 12.1–3) or the belief in an impregnable Zion whose God would be exalted among the nations (Ps. 46). And just as mythology had informed many of these old beliefs, so it was pressed into service to illumine the glorious future which in days to come the prophets in their visions saw descending upon the chosen people. Only it could supply the vocabulary for the miracles which God would accomplish in these days.

Thus Isaiah, after forecasting the coming of a 'shoot from the stump of Jesse', speaks of the renewal of nature's harmony which will accompany his reign:

> The wolf shall dwell with the lamb,
> and the leopard shall lie down with the kid,
> and the calf and the lion and the fatling together,
> and a little child shall lead them ...
> They shall not hurt or destroy
> in all my holy mountain;
> for the earth shall be full of the knowledge of the Lord
> as the waters cover the sea. (Isa. 11.6, 9)

This is clearly a vision of paradise regained (cf. Gen. 2). We may compare the two Isaianic passages (Isa. 2.2–4; 9.6–7) about

Jerusalem and its king quoted earlier; or, without much mythology, Second Isaiah's splendid hope that all the ends of the earth shall turn to Yahweh and be saved (Isa. 45.22–3).

Less eirenic are the many passages which allude to the dawning of a 'day' of the Lord as the harbinger of the divine salvation, with their pictures of violence in nature and of terror and war all around. The day of the Lord had originally been the occasion of Israel's victory in battle, helped by God; it was transmuted by Amos (5.18) into a day of darkness, not of light, to represent the coming judgement in the exile. But later it became a day when God would destroy the godless prior to rescuing those who called on his name; compare Joel 2.1ff., 30ff.

> ... it is near,
> a day of darkness and gloom,
>   a day of clouds and thick darkness!
> Like blackness there is spread upon the mountains
>   a great and powerful people ...
> The earth quakes before them,
>   the heavens tremble ...
> And I will give portents in the heavens and on the earth,
>   blood and fire and columns of smoke.
> The sun shall be turned to darkness,
>   and the moon to blood,
> before the great and terrible day of the Lord comes.

There are other mythologically-tinged pictures of the day of the Lord in Zephaniah, in the latter chapters of Zechariah, and in the final chapter of Malachi.

Related to these visions is the peculiar prophecy of Gog from Magog in Ezekiel chapters 38–9, describing an attack on a restored Israel by the nations of the mysterious north. After ravaging Israel, Gog is itself destroyed and not allowed to affect the peace of its recovery:

> And my holy name I will make known in the midst of my people Israel ... and the nations shall know that I am the Lord, the Holy One in Israel ... That is the day of which I have spoken. (Ezek. 39.7–8)

The future hope of the Old Testament eventually led to the literature called *apocalyptic* (meaning 'unveiling') when, as a result partially of the lowly position of the returning exiles in a world dominated by the great imperial powers of Persia and following them Greece and Rome, all pretence at a historical recovery of the chosen people was abandoned, and a conviction grew that their expectations of universal dominion and peace among the nations would only happen through a divine irruption into history, and its winding up at the end of the times. This literature, with its detailed visions of war in the heavenly places between the forces of good and evil, the final defeat of the devil, the resurrection of the dead, a last judgement, the ultimate triumph of the saints, and the creation of a veritable new heaven and earth, belongs mostly beyond the Old Testament period (for example, in the New Testament Book of Revelation). But it is adumbrated in some late passages in the Old Testament, in Isaiah chapters 24–7, for example, probably the last piece added to the tradition of the Book of Isaiah by disciples, or the second part of the Book of Daniel (chapters 7–12). Myth has come full circle and describes, not the beginning-time, but the end-time, both equally beyond the historical experience of Israel.

A few quotations from these sources must suffice to give a flavour of the heady, but often arcane, rhetoric of the Old Testament in its closing moments:

> On that day the Lord will punish
>   the host of heaven, in heaven,
>   and the kings of the earth, on the earth ...
> Then the moon will be confounded,
>   and the sun ashamed;
> for the Lord of hosts will reign
>   on Mount Zion and in Jerusalem,
> and before his elders he will manifest his glory.
>   (Isa. 24.21, 23)

> In that day the Lord with his hard and great and terrible sword will punish Leviathan the fleeing serpent, Leviathan the twisting serpent, and he will slay the dragon that is in the sea. (Isa. 27.1)

> And behold, with the clouds of heaven
>   there came one like a son of man,

and he came to the Ancient of Days
  and was presented before him.
And to him was given dominion
  and glory and kingdom,
that all peoples, nations, and languages
  should serve him. (Dan. 7.13–14)

At that time shall arise Michael, the great prince who has charge of your people. And there shall be a time of trouble, such as never has been since there was a nation till that time; but at that time your people shall be delivered, every one whose name shall be found written in the book. (Dan. 12.1)

The people of Israel came to their knowledge of the God whom they called Yahweh primarily in the events of their history, but belonging to the age they did, they could not avoid using the language of myth to fill out that knowledge. I have attempted to describe in this chapter some of the chief ways they did that. The mythology they constructed had points of contact with surrounding mythologies, but they always had their experience of God in their own history as a standard of judgement. Their mythology was not permitted to clash with their unique faith, but was used to enhance and enrich it. And it will serve the imaginations of people today in the same way, as long as they do not pretend that there is no myth in the Old Testament, simply because they do not like the term.

-6-

IMAGES OF GOD

M ANY IMAGES OF God have been before us in previous
chapters, in which we discussed the rhetorical features
of the Hebrew language and of the various literary kinds in
which it finds expression in Scripture. In this chapter I gather
these images together, add to their number and attempt a
rough arrangement of them according to the sphere of Israel's
life and experience which they invoke – do they derive from her
mythological thought world, from nature, from statecraft, from
family life and so on? My remarks in Chapters 1 and 2 on the
differences between imaginative and conceptual language, on
the partial and incomplete nature of metaphor, and on the
antiquity, the strangeness and sometimes the unsavouriness of
the society on which the Old Testament writers were dependent for their literary comparisons, still apply. Images are not to
be regarded as doctrines.

God as King

The leading image of God in the Old Testament is undoubtedly
of him as king, and king of the whole universe rather than
merely of Israel. It is in large measure a mythological image
originating, as far as we can tell, in Israel's worship; for it is
commonest in the Psalms and rarest in Israel's historical
records. Perhaps it entered Israel's thinking via the ceremonies
of the temple, which was built after David captured Jerusalem
from the Jebusites, a Canaanite people, though there is evidence
in Judges 8.23 that the nation was acquainted with the kingship
of God before it was in human terms a monarchy. This at any
rate is the implication of Gideon's answer in that verse to those
who offered him a crown: 'I will not rule over you, and my son
will not rule over you; the Lord will rule over you.'

Passages in which God is described as king or as reigning or
ruling have been quoted before, especially in connection with
the mythological themes in Chapter 5.

The following list of new and old quotations may be taken as representative. The little group of Psalms (47, 93, 95–9) known as the 'Enthronement' Psalms is especially important. According to some scholars they formed part of the liturgy at a New Year festival (in Israel in the autumn) when Yahweh was crowned as king, as it were, for another year. Of course, though many are, not every image of God as king is necessarily mythological, some expressing simply his worshippers' devotion and loyalty as they personally experience him:

> Hearken to the sound of my cry,
>   my king and my God ...
> For thou art not a God who delights in wickedness;
>   evil may not sojourn with thee. (Ps. 5.2, 4)

> The voice of the Lord is upon the waters;
>   the God of glory thunders,
>   the Lord, upon many waters ...
> The Lord sits enthroned over the flood;
>   the Lord sits enthroned as king for ever. (Ps. 29.3, 10)

> Yet God my King is from of old,
>   working salvation in the midst of the earth ...
> Thou didst crush the heads of Leviathan ...
> Thou hast fixed all the bounds of the earth. (Ps. 74.12, 14, 17)

> For the Lord is a great God,
>   and a great King above all gods.
> In his hand are the depths of the earth;
>   the heights of the mountains are his also.
> The sea is his, for he made it;
>   for his hands formed the dry land. (Ps. 95.3–5)

> Say among the nations, 'The Lord reigns!
>   Yea, the world is established, it shall never be moved.'
>   (Ps. 96.10)

> The Lord has established his throne in the heavens,
>   and his kingdom rules over all.
> Bless the Lord, O you his angels,
>   you mighty ones who do his word,
> hearkening to the voice of his word!

Bless the Lord, all his hosts,
>   his ministers that do his will!
Bless the Lord, all his works,
>   in all places of his dominion.
Bless the Lord, O my soul! (Ps. 103.19–22)

And I said: 'Woe is me! For I am lost; for I am a man of unclean lips, and I dwell in the midst of a people of unclean lips; for my eyes have seen the King, the Lord of hosts!' (Isa. 6.5)

On that day there shall be neither cold nor frost. And there shall be continuous day ... On that day living waters shall flow out from Jerusalem ... And the Lord will become king over all the earth. (Zech. 14.6–9)

Other images connected with God's kingship

The common titles of God – 'the Lord' (*Adonai*), read instead of Yahweh whenever it appears in Scripture; 'God Most High' (*El Elyon*); and 'God Almighty' (*El Shaddai*) – reflect or at least go well with the notion of God as king. El is the name of the chief Canaanite god, but was not thought dangerous as a general term for 'god' or even as a name for Yahweh, whereas Baal (also meaning 'lord, master, husband') was never used of Yahweh (compare Hosea 2.16ff., where there is a play on words involving its meaning 'husband'). More substantive 'kingly' images are expressed in the epithets Warrior, Judge, and the Living God. On Lord of hosts see Chapter 5, p. 107.

The divine warrior

To the distress of many today, the Old Testament is a very bloodthirsty book, and its God is involved up to his neck. Even in heaven he has his army (hosts), which often fights for his people on earth, and in Israel's early days warfare against neighbouring peoples was divinely sanctioned in the appalling institution of Holy War, in which the soldiers prepared themselves ritually. Yahweh threw the enemy into a panic, delivered them into their hand, and enjoined the slaughter of at least all males or, if the enemy's territory was part of Israel's patrimony, of all the inhabitants and their animals. See the laws of war in

Deuteronomy chapter 20. The savagery of these laws is poignantly illustrated in 1 Samuel 15.10ff., where the kingship is
removed from Saul because he held back some of the booty
which should have been slaughtered; and in 2 Samuel 11.14ff.
where David is forced to act in the light of Uriah's insistence
(though a foreign mercenary) on abstaining from sexual inter-
course before a battle in his plan to get rid of him. Later there is
a change of emphasis in the writing prophets; the threat of
Yahweh's wars was turned against Israel because they had
turned against him; the summoning of foreign armies to punish
Israel was still the divine will. And it continued to be his will
in Israel's eschatological hopes, which saw holy war being
waged beyond history against all evil forces that opposed his
will until he finally ushered in his eternal kingdom.

There are many touching descriptions in the Old Testament
of peace after war, which show peace, not war, as God's
ultimate desire, not only for his own people, but for the
whole world, for example, Micah 4.3–4 (cf. Isa. 2.2–4):

> He shall judge between many peoples,
>   and shall decide for strong nations afar off;
> and they shall beat their swords into ploughshares,
>   and their spears into pruning hooks;
> nation shall not lift up sword against nation,
>   neither shall they learn war any more;
> but they shall sit every man under his vine and under his
>   fig tree,
>   and none shall make them afraid;
> for the mouth of the Lord of hosts has spoken.

But these passages have a hard task to mitigate, far less replace,
the atmosphere of fighting and warfare which pervades the Old
Testament's language, not least its language about their God.
Some examples:

> The Lord is a man of war;
>   the Lord is his name. (Exod. 15.3)

> And Deborah said to Barak, 'Up! For this is the day in which
> the Lord has given Sisera into your hand. Does not the Lord
> go out before you?' (Judg. 4.14)

Images of God

Who is the King of glory?
　The Lord, strong and mighty,
　　the Lord, mighty in battle! (Ps. 24.8)

Blessed be the Lord, my rock,
　who trains my hands for war,
　　and my fingers for battle. (Ps. 144.1)

The Lord goes forth like a mighty man,
　like a man of war he stirs up his fury;
he cries out, he shouts aloud,
　he shows himself mighty against his foes. (Isa. 42.13)

Then the Lord will go forth and fight against those nations as
when he fights on a day of battle. (Zech. 14.3)

God as judge

The idea of God as judge, especially in the Last Judgement, is
usually thought of today as a rather frightening one, and it is so
sometimes in the Old Testament. In the prophetic writings Israel
is condemned for her backsliding, and the sentence of exile
looms ahead; and there are some awesome pictures of God's
arrival in the more distant future. But at other times the appeals
to 'judge' me as an individual or us as a chosen people are
prayers for a favourable verdict or for victory or vindication;
God is assumed to be on Israel's side and his punishments are
for the wicked or for other nations. This may have something to
do with Israel's perception of the law as part of the covenant, a
gift of God, to be therefore accepted with gratitude and even
with love (Pss. 1.2; 119.97) and relied upon as evidence of his
benevolence. There is certainly no trace in the Old Testament of
the suspicion of the law as in opposition to God's grace so
prominent in the teaching of Paul in the New Testament; rather
it is a mark of God's grace. At any rate, the appearance of God as
judge can, however surprising to us, be something to be
welcomed and celebrated, especially in the language of worship.

The two contradictory images of God as judge are illustrated
by the following quotations:

'Shall not the Judge of all the earth do right?' (Gen. 18.25)
(Abraham remonstrates with God on behalf of Sodom and
Gomorrah.)

... the Lord, the Judge, decide this day between the people of Israel and the people of Ammon ... So Jephthah crossed over to the Ammonites to fight against them; and the Lord gave them into his hand. (Judg. 11.27, 32)

Vindicate (AV 'judge') me, O God, and defend my cause
against an ungodly people. (Ps. 43.1)

Let the heavens be glad, and let the earth rejoice;
let the sea roar, and all that fills it;
let the field exult, and everything in it!
Then shall all the trees of the wood sing for joy
before the Lord, for he comes,
for he comes to judge the earth.
He will judge the world with righteousness,
and the peoples with his truth. (Ps. 96.11–13; cf. 98.4–9)

Behold, I send my messenger to prepare the way before me, and the Lord whom you seek will suddenly come to his temple; ... But who can endure the day of his coming, and who can stand when he appears? For he is like a refiner's fire and like fuller's soap; ... Then I will draw near to you for judgment. (Mal. 3.1–2, 5)

The living God

The title is not all that common, though there are many statements that God lives (e.g. Ps. 18.46; Job 19.25), and the oath 'As God lives', 'As I live' is frequently used. In a general sense the title (and the other phrases) celebrate God as the source of life, who gives it and can withdraw it, who saves people from death's approach so that they can rejoin the land of the living (Ps. 116.8–9; Isa. 38.18–19), who sets before Israel the choice of life and death, the one bringing blessing, the other curse (Deut. 30.19–20). In a similar sense the psalmist longs for the living God as a deer for flowing streams (Ps. 42.1) and, like the sparrow, wishes that he could live in the courts of the Lord, where his heart and flesh could sing to the living God (Ps. 84.1–4). But some of the references have a polemical intent, contrasting Yahweh and the gods of their enemy, who cannot deliver their people. Thus David of Goliath:

'... For who is this uncircumcised Philistine, that he should defy the armies of the living God?' (1 Sam. 17.26)

and thus King Hezekiah of Sennacherib:

Incline thy ear, O Lord, and hear ... hear the words of Sennacherib, which he has sent to mock the living God. (2 Kings 19.16)

Compare Jeremiah's call to Israel not to learn the ways of the nations or be afraid of their gods, who are mere idols:

But the Lord is the true God;
    he is the living God and the everlasting King.
At his wrath the earth quakes,
    and the nations cannot endure his indignation. (Jer. 10.10)

This polemic cannot be unconnected with the insults which Elijah directs against the prophets of Baal at Carmel:

And at noon Elijah mocked them, saying, 'Cry aloud, for he is a god; either he is musing, or he has gone aside, or he is on a journey, or perhaps he is asleep and must be awakened.' ... And as midday passed, they raved on until the time of the offering of the oblation, but there was no voice; no one answered, no one heeded. (1 Kings 18.27, 29)

As the Canaanite god of the atmosphere and storm, Baal was supposed to 'die' or 'go to sleep' in the long, hot summer and to 'revive' or 'awake' with the rains of autumn. But Yahweh did not die; he was awake and active at all times.

That occasionally Yahweh was accused of sleeping by his own worshippers and urgently called upon to 'awake' and come to their aid, derives from the same imaginative background (e.g. Ps. 44.23 'Rouse thyself! Why sleepest thou, O Lord?'; Isa. 51.9 'Awake, awake, put on strength, O arm of the Lord') and shows them at their most desperate. He was not supposed to be absent like Baal when his people needed him, for was he not the living God, always available to help them? Perhaps in this light the three-fold repetition in Psalm 121.3-4:

... he who keeps you will not slumber.
Behold, he who keeps Israel
will neither slumber nor sleep

is not so much confident as a little querulous.

The Old Testament and nature

To get the flavour of the Old Testament's attitude to what we call nature (it is not a biblical word) let us look briefly at Psalm 104. It is in effect saying in poetic language what Genesis chapter 1 says in its more theologically studied prose. It begins as does Genesis 1 with light, but it is God's garment, not something that arose in darkness by God's *fiat*. Likewise the heavens are God's tent, the clouds his chariot, the winds his messengers; and the fierce chaos waters, which Genesis 1.2 tries to divest of their menace, in this poem flee headlong at his rebuke. But the end result is the same, the emergence of cosmos out of chaos. From verse 10 onwards it is not the original chaos but God's ongoing and plentiful provision in the world of nature that comes to the fore.

It is particularly noticeable in this poem that humankind is hardly mentioned; God gives wine to gladden their heart and oil to make their face shine (verse 15), but its chief interest is in the birds, the wild goats, the rock badger (or conies (AV); RSV wrongly omits the epithet 'rock'), the beasts of the forest, and the lions, all chosen intentionally, one could almost think, because they live far away from the normal haunts of human beings or are a threat to them – yet God cares for them. Thus subtly is the so-called crown of creation in Genesis 1, humanity (man and woman together) made in God's image, put in its place as but one among his other creatures. See also Job chapters 38 and 39.

Notice too the delightful touches in verse 21, where the lion cubs cry out to God for their food, just like the afflicted souls for deliverance in the lamentation psalms, and in verse 26, where Leviathan is a rather emasculated monster sporting playfully in the sea; no doubt the name is used to describe the whale, but how nice the irony to listeners accustomed to Leviathan as an embodiment of chaos and evil! Verses 27–30 summarize the themes – all things depend on God, not only for sustenance, but for life itself.

But perhaps the most significant point is that in Psalm 104 there is nothing to suggest that nature is anything other than God's creation. There is no pantheism or divinization of nature of the kind we meet in the Lakeland Poets. If the truth were told, the nature poetry of Psalm 104 is about God rather than nature. It is not celebrated for its own sake, but only as the handiwork of God. So in other places. Nature speaks of God without words (cf. Ps. 19.1–3) in the way that a painting tells us something about what kind of person the artist is, but no more. God is not in it (cf. 1 Kings 19.11–12, 'the Lord was not in the wind; …'). The rich imagery drawn from nature with its mythological allusions, its personifications, its exaggerations, its vivid metaphors is never allowed to affect this basic insight. Considering the exposure of Israel's writers to surrounding nature religions, the manner in which this insight is preserved is nothing short of uncanny.

Used to nature poetry of the sort that Wordsworth wrote and indeed deeply affected by it, people of today find it difficult to distinguish the very different kind of nature poetry that the Bible gives us. But distinguish the two we must, if we are to grasp what informs the scriptural view of nature. There is no sentimentality in it, no cloying devotion to domestic pets, no feeling that one is nearer God's heart in a garden than anywhere else on earth, no confusion, in short, between nature and its maker. Human beings share the same maker, and are not above nature but part of it, and must not exploit it. Nature, like them, derives its worth from God.

Naturalistic images of God

In this section I describe some of the ways by which in its figurative language the Old Testament compares God with his created world.

God and the violence of nature

When the Old Testament thinks of God in terms of the natural world, it is most often nature at its fiercest that strikes the writers, as they use storm and thunder to point up his greatness as their creator who can bring them to book. Much of this imagery of upheaval and noise is mythological in origin, as we saw (with plenty of examples) in the last chapter; its extravagance is hardly simply by dint of Israel's observation, though cf. Psalm 107.23ff. with its magnificent picture of a storm at sea and the Lord rescuing the sailors when they cried to him.

Perhaps a word can be added here about God's *spirit*, not exactly an image of God, but it denotes God in action and in not a few cases, especially in the earlier literature, it carries evidence of its concrete, everyday meaning of 'wind'. In Genesis 1.2 it denotes ('moving') the activity of God in opposing the primaeval chaos. In Psalm 139.7 God's spirit is tantamount to his presence, but as a kind of 'hound of heaven' whom the psalmist tries to escape:

> Whither shall I go from thy Spirit?
> Or whither shall I flee from thy presence?

God also sends his spirit to possess human beings, and some of the verbs are worth noting; it 'comes mightily upon' Samson (Judg. 14.6); it 'falls upon' Ezekiel and 'lifts him up' (Ezek. 3.12); and as a result they are able to do marvellous things. Later there is a tendency to tone down the violence, as God 'puts' his spirit 'upon' (Isa. 42.1) or the spirit 'fills' (Exod. 31.3) or 'rests upon' (Isa. 11.2), but even then movement is difficult to dissociate from its operations.

God as shepherd

Due to Psalm 23, the figure of God as a shepherd and his people as sheep is probably the best-known metaphor in the Old Testament. It gives a detailed picture of shepherding in Palestine at the time. Like Joseph's brothers (Gen. 37.12ff.) the shepherd has to traverse long distances to find suitable pasture, looking for water that is still (sheep will not drink from a running stream); he leads them in straight paths; when the way is through dark valleys (probably 'shadow of death' should be translated 'valley of darkness'; there is no necessary reference to death, though as in the case of 'beauty of holiness' a well-loved phrase is thus removed from the Bible) he protects them. His rod is for beating off wild animals (compare the boy

David in 1 Sam. 17.34–5) and presumably his staff or crook for rescuing sheep who had got themselves entangled among the rocks. In English translation the phrases 'he restores my soul' and 'paths of righteousness' should be rendered 'he revives my life' and 'straight paths', as the primary reference is to sheep and only the metaphorical to Israel or human beings.

The picture changes in verse 5 to a banquet scene, where the worshipper is the guest ('anointing' with oil is a common courtesy at table; the word is not the same as that used for the coronation of kings, and there is no allusion to the Messiah), although some have argued that it may refer to the treatment of the sheep after they have returned to the fold. God's house then becomes the fold. It is difficult on either interpretation to explain 'in the presence of my enemies', which rather spoils the idyllic atmosphere (wild animals outside the sheepfold? personal enemies who happen to be in the congregation?), but mercifully it is just a hint, and the idea is not developed (see Chapter 4) for the origin of psalms of trust from the lament genre, in which the enemies of the psalmist play a fuller role).

There are brief allusions to God as shepherd in Psalm 80.1 and Jeremiah 31.10, and in the touching lines in Isaiah 40.11 to God leading his exiles (sheep) home; but in Ezekiel 34 we have a lengthy allegory based on shepherding. The leaders of the nation are removed from their posts, and God himself becomes his people's shepherd, gathering them from the countries where they had been exiled and bringing them back to their own land. As in Isaiah 40 the picture is a tender one:

> I will seek the lost, and I will bring back the strayed, and I will bind up the crippled, and I will strengthen the weak, and the fat and the strong I will watch over; I will feed them in justice. (Ezek. 34.16)

Sometimes the sheep carry some blame for their situation; see Ezekiel 34.17ff.; see also Isaiah 53.6 'All we like sheep have gone astray; we have turned every one to his own way'. But on the whole they are not portrayed as silly, but with compassion as leaderless and defenceless, and especially as lost or strayed. The emphasis in this image of shepherding is on God searching for them and caring for them.

Some other images of God drawn from nature

As bearing his people on eagles' wings (Exod. 19.4); as an eagle defending its young (Deut. 32.11); as hunting his servant like a lion (Job 10.16); as a lion and as 'birds flying', protecting Jerusalem (Isa. 31.4–5); as a bear or lion lying in wait (Lam. 3.10; cf. Hos. 13.7–8); as life-giving waters or rain (Isa. 55.1, 10; Jer. 2.13); as a rock (Pss. 18.2; 61.1–2).

Family images of God

Comparisons of God to animals are relatively rare; the Old Testament much prefers to compare him to human beings. Anthropomorphisms abound, and God takes to himself with considerable relish human actions and feelings and character traits, the less worthy almost as much as the nice, kindlier ones. On the problems raised by this kind of God-language for modern readers of the Old Testament see the discussion in Chapter 2. In this chapter we have already been exercised by the military character which God so often displays. Less controversial might be thought the images drawn from family and clan life treated in this section, but that is only partially true. Images of God as father, as husband, as redeemer have their problems too; the first and the third especially are apt to be misunderstood by today's readers.

God as father (and mother)

In contrast to the New Testament or to later Jewish writings the image of God as father is rather frugally employed in the Old Testament. No doubt this was because in neighbouring religions it tended to be interpreted too literally.

Twice there is an emphasis on God's discipline of us:

> The Lord reproves him whom he loves,
> as a father the son in whom he delights.
> (Prov. 3.12; cf. Deut. 8.5)

And several times he reproaches Israel for rebelling against him, when they should have known better:

Do you thus requite the Lord,
   you foolish and senseless people?
Is not he your father, who created you ...? (Deut. 32.6)

   I thought you would call me, My Father,
      and would not turn from following me. (Jer. 3.19)

   A son honours his father ... If then I am a father, where is my
   honour? (Mal. 1.6)

But much more often it is God's compassion that is emphasized:

   Father of the fatherless and protector of widows
      is God in his holy habitation. (Ps. 68.5)

   As a father pities his children,
      so the Lord pities those who fear him.
   For he knows our frame;
      he remembers that we are dust. (Ps. 103.13–14)

   With weeping they shall come,
      and with consolations I will lead them back ...
   for I am a father to Israel,
      and Ephraim is my first-born. (Jer. 31.9)

   When Israel was a child, I loved him,
      and out of Egypt I called my son. (Hos. 11.1)

They shall be mine, says the Lord of hosts, my special
possession on the day when I act (AV wrongly, but attract-
ively: 'that day when I make up my jewels'), and I will spare
them as a man spares his son who serves him. (Mal. 3.17)

So much for the oft-repeated jibe that the God of the Old
Testament is a strict and unbending father figure. He can be
severe, angry, possessive, even cruel, but it is not as father that
he is so.

But even more remarkable and usually ignored and hardly
noticed (one wonders why) are not a few mother images that
are used of God. In view of the fact that the Old Testament will
have no truck with a goddess, these transferences of feminine

functions and attitudes to a male god are not a little daring; thus:

> You were unmindful of the Rock that bore you,
>> and you forgot the God who gave you birth. (Deut. 32.18)

> But I have calmed and quieted my soul,
>> like a child quieted at its mother's breast. (Ps. 131.2)

>> now I will cry out like a woman in travail,
>> I will gasp and pant. (Isa. 42.14)

>> Hearken to me, O house of Jacob ...
>> who have been borne by me from your birth,
>>> carried from the womb. (Isa. 46.3)

> Can a woman forget her sucking child,
>> that she should have no compassion on the son of
>> her womb?
> Even these may forget,
>> yet I will not forget you. (Isa. 49.15)

>> As one whom his mother comforts,
>>> so I will comfort you. (Isa. 66.13)

God is never addressed as mother as he is (though not often) as father; but the Old Testament does the next best thing. By having God travail with, give birth to, carry his folk from the the womb, dandle them at the breast, it subverts from within, perhaps even without realizing it, the anti-female prejudice so evident in its pages elsewhere. These passages should attract the attention of theologians more than they do, if they wish truly to describe the God of the Old Testament in all his fullness. We certainly have evidence in them and in the majority of kindly father images to justify us in describing the Old Testament God as a motherly father.

God as husband

The figure of God as Israel's husband is only found in the prophets. In Jeremiah 3.20 Israel is pictured as a faithless wife leaving her husband, the context making it clear that it was because she preferred to play the harlot 'on every high hill and under every green tree' (3.6), following Baal and other false lovers; the prophet pleads with her to acknowledge her guilt. Second Isaiah characteristically, at the end of the exile, thinks rather of Israel's return:

> For your Maker is your husband, ...
> For a brief moment I forsook you,
>   but with great compassion I will gather you. (Isa. 54.5, 7)

In Hosea 1.2–9 the prophet is commanded by God to marry a certain Gomer, who was a harlot, and to give symbolic names to their children – Not pitied and Not my people. In actuality he probably found out Gomer's true character after the marriage, and then saw God's hand in it. At any rate he made his own marriage into a type of Israel's betrayal of God and of her fate for her dalliance with Baal religion. Gomer is put away by Hosea, but then he takes her back, because in her love for her he cannot let her go, 'even as the Lord loves the people of Israel, though they turn to other gods and love cakes of raisins' (3.1). Again he sees the parallel with God. Their children will be renamed, 'I will have pity on Not pitied, and I will say to Not my people, "You are my people"' (2.23). This is how he behaves. The whole book thereafter is a bitter polemic against the worship of Baal; there is fierce condemnation, but as in the prophet's own case, Yahweh is unable to allow anger and punishment to have the last word:

> How can I give you up, O Ephraim!
>   How can I hand you over, O Israel! ...
> I will not execute my fierce anger,
>   I will not again destroy Ephraim;
> for I am God and not man,
>   the Holy One in your midst,
>   and I will not come to destroy. (11.8–9)

Finally, a similar message comes through in two long and complicated allegories in Ezekiel. In chapter 16 there is the story of the foundling child (Israel, of course) found by Yahweh, cared for and eventually married by him; but she too played the harlot with her lustful neighbours. In chapter 23 the parable is of the two sisters, Oholah and Oholibah (representing the northern and the southern kingdoms), who became

Yahweh's, but then abandoned him and 'doted upon' their lovers among foreign nations, all 'desirable young men' (Ezek. 23.12). However, Ezekiel is tougher than Hosea, and only in the case of the former foundling is much said about God's forgiveness. Ezekiel's language is a lot cruder and less pleasant than Hosea's; his 'husband' lacks the compassion and warmth of Hosea's (or Second Isaiah's); but there is no doubt of the horror felt by both prophets at Israel's prostitution of her faith. She was treated by her husband far better than she deserved.

God as redeemer

There is a great gulf between the New Testament's understanding of the word 'redeemer' and the Old Testament's. The equivalent Greek noun and verb nearly always denote the believer's salvation through Christ from sin or some alien spiritual power (cf. Gal. 3.13; Eph. 1.7; Titus 2.14; 1 Pet. 1.18). In the Old Testament, on the other hand, only once does the verb refer to the forgiveness of sins (in Ps. 130.8). Elsewhere noun or verb are used of God in deliverance of his people from bondage in Egypt (Exod. 6.6; 15.13; Pss. 77.15; 106.10) or from slavery in exile (Isa. 43.1; 44.22–3; 51.10–11; 52.9) or from some general trouble (Ps. 25.22). Compare:

> I am the Lord, and I will bring you out from under the burdens of the Egyptians, and I will deliver you from their bondage, and I will redeem you with an outstretched arm ... (Exod. 6.6)

> Sing, O heavens, for the Lord has done it;
> shout, O depths of the earth;
> break forth into singing, O mountains,
> O forest, and every tree in it!
> For the Lord has redeemed Jacob,
> and will be glorified in Israel. (Isa. 44.23)

God also redeems individuals, often from mortal illness (Ps. 49.15; Hos. 13.14), but also from the reproach of widowhood (Isa. 54.5), from the unjust treatment meted out to orphans (Prov. 23.10–11), from the malice of persecutors (Ps. 119.154), from imprisonment in a pit (Lam. 3.58); but nowhere from sin, not even in the celebrated passage in Job 19.25, 'I know that my

Redeemer lives'. Rather, Job is making a ringing declaration, on the lines of the confidence pieces in the lamentation psalms, that in spite of all that seems to the contrary, God will see to it that his reputation for integrity, so impugned by the friends and so ignored by God himself, will be salvaged; his erstwhile divine enemy will appear to him, even if only after his death, and he will know that God is on his side (verse 27); moreover God will take his stand on earth (verse 25) (or it may be, over his grave) and declare him innocent for all to hear. His redeemer will not grant him forgiveness of his sins, but vindication against calumny, including his own; and in the end Job's persistence wins the day, though at the time he can scarcely believe it ('My heart faints within me!' (verse 27)). It is not to be wondered at that Christian readers, mesmerized by the New Testament's interpretation of redemption and with the strains of Handel's soprano aria from the thoroughly Christianized *Messiah* ringing in their ears, get the passage hopelessly wrong.

Redemption in the Old Testament derives from a secular source, from Old Israelite family or clan law, where the redeemer (in Hebrew *goel*) is the technical term for the nearest male relative who is obliged to buy back property so that it may be kept within the family (Lev. 25.25–34), or to ransom a kinsman from slavery (Lev. 25.47–55), or to marry a relative's widow so that an heir may be provided for her dead husband (Ruth 4.1–6), or to avenge the blood of a murdered kinsman (Deut. 19.11–13; 2 Sam. 14.4–11). As used of God, therefore, its proper meaning is to do a kinsman's duty towards his people and to rescue them from ruination or disaster or false accusation. In terms of an individual's or Israel's salvation it involves much more than saving them from sin; it means saving them from any kind of trouble, simply because he is their kinsman. It has little to do with a worshipper's sin, except in so far as that can land him in distress; it is his need that elicits the help of his divine redeemer or kinsman.

There are many other images of God which we have not detailed in this chapter. Quite common, for instance, are those based on Palestinian trades or professions. God is compared many times to a teacher (Ps. 119.33; Isa. 28.26), not a few times to a potter (Isa. 45.9; 64.8), occasionally to a husbandman (Isa. 5.2), a smelter (Isa 1.25), a builder (Ps. 147.2), a physician (Ps. 103.3), a harvester (Jer 8.13), and so on. In this chapter I have concentrated on some of the more frequently recurring images – those related to God's kingship and those drawn from the natural world and from family life. Many have delighted us, some have surprised us, some have perturbed us. But that hardly matters. They give us an impression of how ancient Israel conceived God, not of course as he is in himself: and that cannot but broaden our own faith, as long as we remember that our images of God, which we tend to think are superior, are equally partial. The time for knowing him is not yet, but in another life.

−7−

IMAGES OF HUMANITY

THE PICTURE OF human beings that emerges from the Old Testament is a sombre one. This is only to be expected in a body of writings which is chiefly concerned with their need of salvation and with the kind of God who saves them. It is not greatly softened by their being described in Genesis 1.26 as created in the 'image' of God. Most interpreters have taken this verse too positively, failing to grasp the kind of language in which it is formulated.

What does the 'image' really mean?

Much of Genesis chapter 1 relates the creation of the world in terms of primitive science – flat earth, firmament up there, and so on – but the passage in verses 26–31 about the creation of human beings is not primitive science. Rather it states in quite figurative language what in the view of the chapter's priestly authors was God's purpose in their creation. It was, put bluntly, to be God's 'image' in ruling his creation for him. But the figure of the 'image' is an extremely daring one; and this should give us pause before assuming that, against the Old Testament's view elsewhere, it sets the human race on some kind of pedestal.

The Hebrew word is not the same as the one used in the second commandment (Exod. 20.4), 'You shall not make for yourself a graven image, or any likeness that is in heaven above...', nor is the word 'likeness'; but they are both sufficiently near in meaning to the Exodus words to have those listening wondering what the authors of Genesis could possibly be getting at. The Genesis word 'image' appears in Numbers 33.52 of the destruction of Canaanite idols and in 2 Kings 11.18 of the breaking in pieces of idols of Baal. Similarly, the Genesis word 'likeness' is predicated of God in Isaiah 40.18–19:

> To whom then will you liken God,
> or what likeness compare with him?

> The idol! a workman casts it,
>   and a goldsmith overlays it with gold,
>   and casts for it silver chains.

This obviously implies that he should not be compared with any visible counterpart. On the surface both could have been used in the second commandment, and both seem eminently unsuitable to enhance the standing of human beings.

Perhaps a paraphrase will help us to get behind the authors' intention. They are, in the most pungent and arresting manner they could think of, saying two things about human beings. First they say: 'You know that to those foolish enough to bow down before it, an idol represents a non-existent pagan deity. Well, the one true God has – if you will pardon the word – his image too, only that image is not a block of stone but we humans. We represent him on earth. But we are not, of course, blocks of stone. We represent him in other ways than by simply being there.' And second they say: 'You know that we cannot really describe God, but in fact we often speak of him in human terms, as though he did in fact talk to us, ask us to do things, was pleased or angry with us, and so on. In that limited sense you could say he is "like us" or that we were made "after his likeness".' The first word is not speaking of humanity's nature but of their status, and the second one must therefore mean that only in that way, and not in themselves, can they be said to resemble God.

The harsh verbs in which their status is spelt out should also be taken with a pinch of salt and the paradox and exaggeration involved in them appreciated.

The first verb, Hebrew *radah* (Gen. 1.26, 28), is much stronger than the RSV's 'have dominion' or the NEB's 'rule' or even 'master'. It is used in 1 Kings 9.23 of Solomon's overseers levying the forced labour needed to build the temple; and in Isaiah 14.2 of Israel defeating her oppressors and turning the tables on them. 'Dominate' or 'lord it over' would be more accurate English equivalents. The second verb, Hebrew *kabash* (Gen. 1.28), translated 'subdue', means literally to 'trample on'. It is used in Zechariah 9.15 of Israel treading down in the last days the weapons (or the soldiery) of her vanquished enemies; and in Jeremiah 34.11 of the burghers of Jerusalem grabbing back their slaves after having released them during the

Babylonian invasion of Judah. 'Subjugate' has the correct nasty nuance.

A sensitive Hebrew would recall that Psalm 8 contains similar thoughts but shows amazement at them, thus in effect warning the unwary interpreter:

> What is man that thou art mindful of him,
>   and the son of man that thou dost care for him?
> Yet thou hast made him little less than God,
>   and dost crown him with glory and honour.
> Thou hast given him dominion over the works of thy hands;
>   thou hast put all things under his feet. (verses 4–6)

For 'little less than God' the AV has 'a little lower than the angels' which, as God is the subject, is preferable: the Hebrew word is *elohim*, which means 'divine beings' or even 'gods' as well as 'God' (e.g. Ps. 82.1). The phrase is the equivalent of Genesis's 'Let us make man in our image', which with its plural 'us' and 'we' is likewise reluctant to compare human beings directly with God, but hides God among his angelic host just at this significant moment. Both texts are being very subtle. It is a pity that most interpreters have not shown a similar subtlety in discussing the image. They argue over which element in human beings might constitute it – their freewill, their ability to speak, their reasoning capacity, and so on – whereas the two Hebrew texts which they are supposed to be interpreting are intentionally toning down the literal sense of what they are saying.

The statement in Psalm 8 'dost crown him' perhaps gives us our clue. All the vocabulary used in both texts describing how the image shows itself is autocratic; it is kingly language. But in the context of creation only God is king. Such power as human beings possess over the rest of creation must have been given them by him. It is described in typical Hebrew hyperbole as the power of a despot, a taskmaster, or a king because it is ultimately God's power. Human beings could only use it rightly if they used it as God himself would use it; there is also the unwritten implication that they will one day have to give an account of their stewardship, and will have not a little difficulty in justifying themselves.

What a travesty that these verses in Genesis chapter 1 have

been read so literalistically by many, especially in the developed world, and that the calculated but nonetheless figurative language that is employed has gone so unperceived. They have fired the ambition and arrogance of human beings when they should have done the very opposite. Properly understood, Genesis chapter 1 is not claiming a superiority for human beings over the rest of creation that in any way brings them in their nature nearer to God; nor is it giving them *carte blanche* to exploit the created world for their own ends. Like the rest of creation they are made by God and are equally dependent on him. If they have been given something special, it is a functional role which does not affect their creatureliness; and considering the way they behave, it is a task in which they are not doing well.

What is the knowledge of good and evil?

We can safely say that the knowledge of good and evil is not moral discrimination nor is it the ability to distinguish what is beneficial from what is harmful. How could God wish to withhold such kinds of knowledge from human beings? A phrase in 2 Samuel 14.17 hints at the correct interpretation. In this passage the wise woman of Tekoa praises Absalom for having wisdom 'like the angel of God to discern good and evil'. A little later (14.20) she says, obviously meaning the same thing, that he has wisdom 'like the angel of God to know all things that are on the earth'. The phrase 'good and evil' means in Hebrew something like our English expression 'good, bad and indifferent'. It is a colourful way of saying 'everything'.

It is therefore the kind of knowledge that belongs to divinity, to the angels and thus ultimately to God himself, that is forbidden to humanity, the kind of full and comprehensive knowledge that brings to its possessor power and independence. Human beings are being told that they must not set their sights on a divine status that is not their's to possess, but should remember their creatureliness and their dependence upon God in all things.

Of course, the story of the Garden is a myth. It is not suggesting that human beings were once bereft of this kind of knowledge, but that they already acquired it in aiming at divinity. And herein lies their sin, the canker at the heart of the human condition. This is a hard message for our modern age to swallow when the insatiable search for knowledge is universally commended. We are in the habit of arguing that the possession of knowledge should be distinguished from the use to which people put it. The author of Genesis 2 and 3 does not make any such distinction, and would regard it as evading the issue. To him the knowledge of good and evil and of sin are inextricably bound up together in the human constitution. As human beings cultivate the one so they fall into the other.

Human sin

The sinfulness of humanity as a whole is traced in Genesis to their turning away from God and trying to live without him. It is, however, the sins of Israel, his special people, that predominate in the Old Testament. These presuppose a believing people, but they are nonetheless human sins which share in the condemnation of the whole human race. Israel's hands too are usurping hands, though they should have known better.

Perhaps the sins which bulk largest are ingratitude, apostasy, and social injustice. See, for examples, Chapter 4 on the satire of Amos at the expense of a selfish and uncaring nation, and on the foolish actions of people and the consequences they draw in their wake, Chapter 6 on a wife's faithlessness as an image of Israel's failure to be loyal to Yahweh. For fuller lists of actions and attitudes that arise from Israel's propensity to sin see passages like Job 31, Psalms 15 and 51, Proverbs 26, Isaiah 1 and 59, Jeremiah 2, Hosea 4, Micah 6. These contain between them many of the varied images which the Old Testament writers had at their disposal in exposing the sins of Israel. The following quotations give us a taste of their rhetoric:

> If I have raised my hand against the fatherless,
>   because I saw help in the gate;
> then let my shoulder blade fall from my shoulder,
>   and let my arm be broken from its socket. (Job 31.21–2)

> Wash me thoroughly from my iniquity,
>   and cleanse me from my sin! (Ps. 51.2)

> He who digs a pit will fall into it,
>   and a stone will come back upon him who starts it rolling.
>   (Prov. 26.27)

The ox knows its owner,
  and the ass its master's crib;
but Israel does not know,
  my people does not understand. (Isa. 1.3)

Though your sins are like scarlet,
  they shall be as white as snow;
though they are red like crimson,
  they shall become like wool. (Isa. 1.18)

They conceive mischief and bring forth iniquity. (Isa. 59.4)

Look at your way in the valley;
  know what you have done –
a restive young camel interlacing her tracks,
  a wild ass used to the wilderness,
in her heat sniffing the wind!
  Who can restrain her lust? (Jer. 2.23–4)

Like a stubborn heifer,
  Israel is stubborn;
can the Lord now feed them
  like a lamb in a broad pasture? (Hos. 4.16)

There is no doubt that the Old Testament regards sin as endemic in the human race, not least in Israel, an inescapable sign of being human, and at least a partial cause, not only of their separation from God, but of their own suffering and misery in this world.

Human creatureliness

Sin and its consequences are not the only ingredient in the human condition. Human beings have to live with their creatureliness, and if one takes the Old Testament as a whole, its imagery reminds them as much of that as of their sinfulness. It is their fate as creatures in God's world that gives rise to the cry of lament so characteristic of the Psalms and the Book of Job, but by no means absent elsewhere. It is sometimes a cry of protest to God for creating the world the way he did; sometimes a cry of innocence in the face of tragedy he has caused; but chiefly it is a cry of despair in the face of his harsh providence, and a cry to him for relief. It is heard as early as Genesis 5.29 where Lamech gives a name to his son Noah (meaning 'rest'), saying:

> Out of the ground which the Lord has cursed this one shall bring us relief from our work and from the toil of our hands.

This plaintive note contrasts him with another Lamech, who in 4.23-4 says to his two wives:

> I have slain a man for wounding me,
>   a young man for striking me.
> If Cain is avenged sevenfold,
>   truly Lamech seventy-sevenfold.

This is the arrogant and vengeful spirit which leads Genesis to trace humanity's baleful lot to their sin (see the punishment on Adam, 3.17, or the prelude to the Flood, 6.5–7); but the cry of the later Lamech is also, often and urgently, taken up in the Old Testament; and though it does not drown the widespread condemnation of human sin, it sometimes comes near to doing so. Creaturely frailty is as much a mark of the human lot as sin; and its description involves a profusion of largely pessimistic images.

There is, first, a cluster of images associating human beings with dust or clay. Right at the beginning Genesis 2.7 reminds us that they were formed of the dust of the ground, and 3.19 equally forcibly that to dust they shall return. Ecclesiastes 3.20 makes essentially the same point: 'All go to one place; all are from the dust, and all turn to dust again.' In Genesis 3.19 the tone is condemnatory (humanity has brought this fate upon themselves); in the Ecclesiastes quote it is pessimistic, but a warmer note is struck in Psalm 103.14, where God's compassion is enlisted by appealing to him as Creator: 'he knows our frame; he remembers that we are dust'.

The image of clay normally operates in a demeaning fashion, as in Job 4.19 where Eliphaz is denying that any human being can be pure in God's sight; God does not even trust his angels, so how can he trust 'those who dwell in houses of clay' (a metaphor of the human body) 'whose foundation is in the dust, who are crushed before (sooner than) the moth'? The same image often spills over into potter/clay comparisons, as in

Isaiah 45.9: 'Does the clay say to him who fashions it, "What are you making?"'

There is a final point worth noticing about the origin of human beings in the dust. In Genesis 2.7 it is called 'dust from the ground', and the word 'ground' gives rise to a play on words. In Hebrew it is *adamah*, which has no etymological connection with the name Adam. But they sound similar; it cannot therefore be by chance that *adamah* is mentioned no less than fourteen times in the story of the Garden and the story of Cain which follows it. Any Hebrew speaker would be bound to notice the link in sound as he read these chapters. Adam's creation from *adamah* is as significant an element in his nature as his disobedience.

A second cluster of images has human beings compared to breath or wind. Job chapter 7 contains a good example:

Remember that my life is a breath; ...
As the cloud fades and vanishes,
   so he who goes down to Sheol does not come up.

(verses 7, 9)

Again in 7.16 we have: 'Let me alone, for my days are a breath.' This chapter of Job is in fact very rich in images of this kind. At the beginning Job speaks of a man's hard service as a conscripted soldier, of his days being like those of a hireling, of a slave longing for evening's shadow, or a hireling waiting for his wages, while in verse 6 his life is compared to a weaver's shuttle. A comparable range of metaphors is found in Hezekiah's thanksgiving for his return after illness to the land of the living (Isa. 38.10ff.).

The same images of breath appear in a number of psalms, for example:

Lord, let me know my end ...
   let me know how fleeting my life is!
Behold, thou hast made my days a few handbreadths,
   and my lifetime is as nothing in thy sight.
Surely every man stands as a mere breath!
   Surely man goes about as a shadow! (Ps. 39.4–6)

Compare Psalms 62.9; 144.4.

One of the Hebrew words for breath is *hebel*, and it is this word which, translated 'vanity', sounds like the striking of a hammer throughout the Book of Ecclesiastes, as the writer pours scorn on human pride and pretension.

But, as we have seen, breath references highlight the short life of human beings as much as they do its 'vanity'. It is the shortness of human life, contrasted with God's eternity, that is emphasized in a third cluster of images, those to do with grass and flowers. The passage at the beginning of Job 14, which used to be read at funerals but is, I would guess, not so often heard in these days, when medical science is frantically and with the approval of all trying to prolong the human life span, is representative:

> Man that is born of a woman is of few days,
> and full of trouble.
> He comes forth like a flower, and withers;
> he flees like a shadow, and continues not.

We get the same image in Psalm 102.11:

> My days are like an evening shadow;
> I wither away like grass.

This psalm also has other poignant images of the human condition – smoke (verse 3), the pelican in the wilderness (AV, verse 6), the sparrow on the housetop (AV, verse 7) – all contrasting human beings with him who, though the earth and the heavens perish, endures and whose years have no end (verses 25ff.).

There are also the well-known passages from Psalm 103.15ff. ('As for man, his days are like grass; he flourishes like a flower of the field; ... But the steadfast love of the Lord is from everlasting to everlasting') or Isaiah 40.6ff. ('All flesh is grass ... but the word of our God will stand for ever').

Isaiah mentions all flesh, and that leads on to a fourth cluster of images in which flesh (as of the earth) is contrasted with spirit (which is divine). Perhaps the strongest statement is Isaiah 31.3, 'The Egyptians are men, and not God; and their horses are flesh, and not spirit.' Compare Jeremiah 17.5ff., 'Cursed is the man who trusts in man, and makes flesh his arm ... He is like a shrub in the desert'. Or there is Hezekiah's declaration of faith as Jerusalem is attacked (2 Chron. 32.8),

'With him (the enemy) is an arm of flesh; but with us is the Lord ... to fight our battles'.

Alongside talk of human sin and rebellion, there is thus a wide variety of pictures in the Old Testament which draw attention to the creaturely frailty of human beings, and in differing ways emphasize their weakness compared with God's power, or their short and fleeting life compared with God's eternity, or their helplessness that has them crying out for God's aid and compassion. But most enduring of all perhaps is the picturing of the human condition as one of toil and trouble and suffering, as in the sentences on Adam and Eve in Genesis 3 which are explained as the result of sin, but as also in Job 5.7 where it is simply stated that 'man is born to trouble as the sparks fly upward', or as in Psalm 90.9–10 where God the Creator is implicated:

> For all our days pass away under thy wrath,
>   our years come to an end like a sigh.
> The years of our life are threescore and ten,
>   or even by reason of strength fourscore;
> yet their span is but toil and trouble;
>   they are soon gone, and we fly away.

Pain and toil and suffering are in the Old Testament not only, or even chiefly, the consequence of sin, but part and parcel of the human lot, the melancholy accompaniment of being human and living on earth as creatures of God. The denizens of the advanced world may take offence at such a gloomy and pessimistic explication of the human condition, but the poor and hungry in the Third World have to endure it, and know how true it is.

Women in the Old Testament

Both in story and poetry women make their mark in Old Testament society. They can achieve high positions and show remarkable strength of character like Rebekah who schemed for her boy (Gen. 27), or Tamar who upstaged her father-in-law (Gen. 38), or Deborah who summoned Israel to war (Judg. 4.5–7), or Naomi who extricated her daughter-in-law from the reproach of widowhood (Ruth), or Queen Esther who rescued her people from one of the earliest pogroms. Proverbs chapter 31 tells of the resourceful housewife, who looked after her family and was praised by her husband in the gate. Rachel was genuinely loved by Jacob; and the Song of Solomon celebrates in sensuous imagery the mutual love of a young man and woman engaged to be married; the girl takes a full part in the exchange of compliments:

> As an apple tree among the trees of the wood,
>   so is my beloved among young men.
> With great delight I sat in his shadow,
>   and his fruit was sweet to my taste.
> He brought me to the banqueting house,
>   and his banner over me was love. (2.3–4)

Yet such happiness and fulfilment as women attained in ancient Israel was attained in spite of a legal system and social customs which discriminated severely against them. Even in the Ten Commandments a wife was included among her husband's possessions along with his slaves or his ox and ass (Exod. 20.17), and she had to call him lord or master as though she were a slave or a king's subject. Neither wife nor daughter could inherit property except when there was no male heir. A man could not sell his wife, though he could his daughter. He could divorce his wife, but not she him.

Her primary role was to supply him with children, especially sons; Psalm 127.3–5:

> Lo, sons are a heritage from the Lord,
>   the fruit of the womb a reward.
> Like arrows in the hand of a warrior are the sons of one's
>   youth.
> Happy is the man who has
>   his quiver full of them!

When she was barren, however, she felt under a curse; see 1 Samuel 1.6, where Hannah's distress at not bearing children is compounded by the taunts of Peninnah, Elkanah's other wife, that 'the Lord had closed her womb'.

And when she was widowed, her fate and that of her children, bereft of male protection, could be pitiable; compare

the widow of Zarephath answering Elijah's request for some
sustenance (1 Kings 17.12):

> As the Lord your God lives, I have nothing baked, only a
> handful of meal in a jar, and a little oil in a cruse; and now, I
> am gathering a couple of sticks, that I may go in and prepare
> it for myself and my son, that we may eat it, and die.

The heartfelt pleas of the prophets commending widows and
orphans to people's charity, and even God's obvious bias in
their favour, though most welcome, simply prove how neglected and ignored they were.

Lastly, female misbehaviour is undoubtedly highlighted in
Old Testament rhetoric. The Book of Proverbs makes rather a lot
of the dangers which the adulteress or the harlot present to the
young scholar (see Chapter 5); and the prophets, especially
Hosea and Ezekiel, the latter in most unpleasant language, use
the figure of an adulterous wife to represent the seductive
worship of Baal (see Chapter 6). Even female foibles and
weaknesses are commonly lampooned, sometimes humorously,
sometimes quite savagely; see Proverbs 11.22 (lack of discre-
tion), 25.24 (noisy argumentativeness), Isaiah 3.16ff. (mincing
walk, fondness of jewels and make-up), Amos 4.1ff. (unfeeling
snobbery). As so often in other societies, our own included,
women are singled out for male jokes and lascivious criticism,
and little account is taken of the hurt this can cause them.

Worst of all are the misinterpretations that have become
attached over the centuries to the story of the Garden of
Eden. Far too often these have debased womankind by
calling on Scripture to justify their subordination to men or to
suggest that their pain in childbirth was God's will. Our
Victorian forefathers even forbad anaesthetics in labour on
the strength of Genesis 3.16, though Genesis 3.17 did not
prevent them hypocritically inventing fertilizers and tractors
to mitigate men's toil in the field. Such interpretations are not
only obscene, but quite ignore the nature of the story as myth
(see Chapter 5). The story speaks of a past instead of a potential
and of God's punishment instead of a human situation which he
has sorrowfully to accept. There never was a time when women
were not considered inferior to men or a time when they did
not suffer in childbirth. It was, in fact, their share in the misery

and trouble that in passage after passage of the Old Testament (see the last section) is the perennial lot of human beings in this 'vale of tears'.

✟ Human life as a way or pilgrimage

The Old Testament is full of the idea of journeying, and it has been taken up by later Jewish and Christian writings to illumine the life of the believing community or individual as they seek a path to follow in the present and as they set before them in hope a goal to be one day attained. The image is encountered in various disguises.

There are first a host of comparisons of life to a road or a way. These are drawn from the circumstances of daily living in a country and in an era without vehicles, when not even riding on a donkey but walking on foot was the usual manner of getting from one place to another. Here are some examples:

Noah walked with God. (Gen. 6.9)

You shall be careful to do therefore as the Lord your God has commanded you; you shall not turn aside to the right hand or to the left. You shall walk in all the way which the Lord your God has commanded you. (Deut. 5.32–3)

And now I am about to go the way of all the earth. (Josh. 23.14)

> Blessed is the man
> who walks not in the counsel of the wicked,
> nor stands in the way of sinners. (Ps. 1.1)

He leads me in paths of righteousness
for his name's sake.
Even though I walk through the valley of the shadow
of death,
I fear no evil;
for thou art with me. (Ps. 23.3–4)

Try me and know my thoughts!
And see if there be any wicked way in me,
and lead me in the way everlasting! (Ps. 139.23–4)

Even youths shall faint and be weary,
  and young men shall fall exhausted;
but they who wait for the Lord shall renew their strength,
  they shall mount up with wings like eagles,
they shall run and not be weary,
  they shall walk and not faint. (Isa. 40.30–1)

    Stand by the roads, and look,
      and ask for the ancient paths,
    where the good way is; and walk in it,
      and find rest for your souls. (Jer. 6.16)

I know, O Lord, that the way of man is not in himself,
  that it is not in man who walks to direct his steps.
                                    (Jer. 10.23)

Why does the way of the wicked prosper? (Jer. 12.1)

    Can two walk together, except they be agreed?
                              (AV Amos 3.3)

Second, there are many forceful and colourful descriptions of
the journeying of Israel's patriarchal ancestors and of Israel's
own forty years' wandering in the wilderness:

And they went forth to go into the land of Canaan; and into
the land of Canaan they came. (AV Gen. 12.5)

And Abram journeyed on, still going toward the Negeb.
(Gen. 12.9)

God led the people round by the way of the wilderness
toward the Red Sea ... And the Lord went before them by
day in a pillar of cloud to lead them along the way, and by
night in a pillar of fire to give them light, that they might
travel by day and by night. (Exod. 13.18, 21)

Not one of these men of this evil generation shall see the
good land which I swore to give to your fathers ... [But] your
little ones, who you said would become a prey, and your
children, who this day have no knowledge of good or evil,
shall go in there ... But as for you, turn, and journey into the
wilderness. (Deut. 1.35, 39–40)

A wandering Aramean (AV: 'a Syrian ready to perish') was my father; and he went down into Egypt ... and the Lord brought us out of Egypt with a mighty hand ... and he brought us into this place and gave us this land, a land flowing with milk and honey. (Deut. 26.5, 8–9)

A third idea related to our theme, which is met with especially in the Psalms, is that of the pilgrimage to Zion, the holy city:

Who shall ascend the hill of the Lord?
    And who shall stand in his holy place?
He who has clean hands and a pure heart... (Ps. 24.3–4)

My soul thirsts for God,
    for the living God.
When shall I come and behold
    the face of God? (Ps. 42.2)

Oh send out thy light and thy truth;
    let them lead me,
let them bring me to thy holy hill,
    and to thy dwelling! (Ps. 43.3)

Blessed are the men whose strength is in thee,
    in whose heart are the highways to Zion. (Ps. 84.5)

I was glad when they said to me,
    'Let us go to the house of the Lord!' (Ps. 122.1)

In some passages the idea of the pilgrimage to Jerusalem is finely interwoven with that of the wilderness wandering, as in the passage below from Isaiah, in which the prophet is looking forward to the return to Zion after exile in Babylon:

The wilderness and the dry land shall be glad,
    the desert shall rejoice and blossom;...
And a highway shall be there,
    and it shall be called the Holy Way;...
And the ransomed of the Lord shall return,
    and come to Zion with singing. (Isa. 35.1, 8, 10)

Put all these passages together – about life as a path or road, about Israel's journey to the Promised Land, about the pilgrimage to Zion – and we have a marvellous mix of images with which to elucidate faith and conduct. They underline that the life of believers is an ongoing process, with a beginning that demands commitment and a goal to aim at, though not yet to attain. They warn believers that all through life there are choices to be made and false turnings to be avoided. And they remind them that they are not alone but have a protector and guide beside them, who has brought them to where they now are and will stay with them till their journey's end.

The praise of God

It may be true that the Old Testament does not give human beings a good press. Nevertheless, especially in the Psalms, where their own voice is heard rather than the instructions and warnings and appeals and promises of the rest of Scripture, there is a strong note of acceptance of this world, and of thanksgiving to God for his creation and providence, for mercies received and sins forgiven, for the joys of true friendship and of family life; above all of praise towards him who made them and set them in the midst of what was still a good earth; and who, when they were gone, would still be there. 'Man's chief end', says the Shorter Scottish Catechism in one of its rare Old Testament moods, 'is to glorify God and enjoy him for ever.' Praise of God is the Old Testament's ultimate balm for the sinful and sorrowful children of men as they pursue their daily pilgrimage to a better place.

FURTHER READING

On the value of literary study in general:

N. Frye, *The Educated Imagination*. Indiana University Press, 8th printing, 1974.

On the scope of Old Testament criticism, with particular reference to literary competence and genre recognition:

J. Barton, *Reading the Old Testament: Method in Biblical Study*. Darton, Longman and Todd 1984.

Books on the literary study of the Bible, with emphasis on the Old Testament:

R. Alter, *The Art of Biblical Narrative*. George Allen and Unwin 1981.
R. Alter, *The Art of Biblical Poetry*. T. & T. Clark 1985.
D. Daiches, *God and the Poets* (Gifford Lectures, 1983). Oxford University Press 1984.
H. Fisch, *Poetry with a Purpose: Biblical Poetics and Interpretation*. Indiana University Press 1980.
T. R. Henn, *The Bible as Literature*. Lutterworth 1970.
C. S. Lewis, *Reflections on the Psalms*. Collins, Fount Paperbacks, 1977.
L. Ryken, *The Literature of the Bible*. Zondervan 1974.
S. Sandmel, *The Enjoyment of Scripture*. Oxford University Press 1972.

On the technical side of Hebrew poetry, notably parallelism:

W. G. E. Watson, *Classical Hebrew Poetry: A Guide to its Techniques*. JSOT Press 1984.

On imagery:

S. J. Brown, *Image and Truth: Studies in the Imagery of the Bible*. Officium Libri Catholici 1955.
G. B. Caird, *The Language and Imagery of the Bible*. Duckworth 1980.

On specific themes:

P. C. Craigie, *The Problem of War in the Old Testament*. Eerdmans 1976.
R. Davidson, *The Courage to Doubt: Exploring an Old Testament Theme*. SCM Press 1983.
J. Day, *God's Conflict with the Dragon and the Sea: Echoes of a Canaanite Myth in the Old Testament*. Cambridge University Press 1985.

Further Reading

E. M. Good, *Irony in the Old Testament*. Westminster Press 1965; The Almond Press 1985.

A. E. Lewis (ed.), *The Motherhood of God*. St Andrew Press 1984.

C. Westermann, *Praise and Lament in the Psalms*. T. & T. Clark 1981.

H. W. Wolff, *Anthropology of the Old Testament*. SCM Press 1974.

Background:

J. C. L. Gibson, *Canaanite Myths and Legends*. T. & T. Clark 1978.

H. Frankfort and others. *Before Philosophy: The Intellectual Adventure of Ancient Man*. Penguin Books 1949.

G. A. Smith, *The Historical Geography of the Holy Land*. 1894; 25th edn 1931; reprinted in Collins, Fontana Library, 1966.

I. J. Stadelmann, *The Hebrew Conception of the World*. Biblical Institute Press 1970.

R. de Vaux, *Ancient Israel: Its Life and Institutions*. Darton, Longman and Todd 1973.

Reference (especially on new influences on and methods of biblical study):

R. J. Coggins & J. L. Houlden (eds.), *A Dictionary of Biblical Interpretation*. SCM Press 1990.

INDEX OF BIBLICAL REFERENCES

Old Testament

New Testament

INDEX OF NAMES AND SUBJECTS